SHURLEY ENGLISH

HOMESCHOOL MADE EASY

LEVEL 3

Student Book

By

Brenda Shurley

Shurley Instructional Materials, Inc., Cabot, Arkansas

07-16
Shurley English Homeschooling
Level 3 Student Workbook
ISBN 978-1-58561-041-9

Printed in the United States of America by RR Donnelley, Harrisonburg, VA.

For additional information or to place an order, write to: Shurley Instructional Materials, Inc.
366 SIM Drive
Cabot, AR 72023

1 2 3 4 5 6 7 8 9 10 11 12   16 15 14 13 11 09 07 06 04 03 01

JINGLE

SECTION

Jingle Section

Jingle 1: Noun Jingle

This little noun
Floating around
Names a person, place, or thing.
With a knick knack, paddy wack,
These are English rules.
Isn't language fun and cool?

Jingle 2: Verb Jingle

A verb shows action,
There's no doubt!
It tells what the subject does,
Like sing and shout.

Action verbs are fun to do.
Now, it's time to name a few.
So, clap your hands
And join our rhyme;
Say those verbs in record time!

Wiggle, jiggle, turn around;
Raise your arms
And stomp the ground.
Shake your finger and wink your eye;
Wave those action verbs good-bye.

Jingle 3: Sentence Jingle

A sentence, sentence, sentence
Is complete, complete, complete
When 5 simple rules
It meets, meets, meets.

It has a subject, subject, subject
And a verb, verb, verb.
It makes sense, sense, sense
With every word, word, word.

Add a capital letter, letter
And an end mark, mark.
Now, we're finished, and aren't we smart!
Now, our sentence has all its parts!

REMEMBER
Subject, Verb, Com-plete sense,
Capital letter, and an end mark, too.
That's what a sentence is all about!

Jingle Section

Jingle 4: Adverb Jingle

An adverb modifies a verb, adjective, or another adverb.
An adverb asks *How? When? Where?*
To find an adverb: **Go, Ask, Get**.
Where do I **go**? To a verb, adjective, or another adverb.
What do I **ask**? How? When? Where?
What do I **get**? An ADVERB! (Clap) (Clap)
That's what!

Jingle 5: Adjective Jingle

An adjective modifies a noun or pronoun.
An adjective asks *What kind? Which one? How many?*
To find an adjective: **Go, Ask, Get**.
Where do I **go**? To a noun or pronoun.
What do I **ask**? What kind? Which one? How many?
What do I **get**? An ADJECTIVE! (Clap) (Clap)
That's what!

Jingle 6: Article Adjective Jingle

We are the article adjectives,
Teeny, tiny adjectives:
A, AN, THE - A, AN, THE.

We are called article adjectives and noun markers;
We are memorized and used every day.
So, if you spot us, you can mark us
With the label A.

We are the article adjectives,
Teeny, tiny adjectives:
A, AN, THE - A, AN, THE.

Jingle Section

Jingle 7: Preposition Jingle

A PREP PREP PREPOSITION
Is a special group of words
That connects a
NOUN, NOUN, NOUN
Or a PRO, PRO, PRONOUN
To the rest of the sentence.

Jingle 8: Object of the Prep Jingle

Dum De Dum Dum!
An O-P is a N-O-U-N or a P-R-O
After the P-R-E-P
In a S-E-N-T-E-N-C-E.
Dum De Dum Dum - DONE!

Jingle 9: Preposition Flow Jingle

1. **Preposition, Preposition Starting with an A.**
(Fast)
aboard, about, above,
across, after, against,
(Slow)
along, among, around, at.

2. **Preposition, Preposition Starting with a B.**
(Fast)
before, behind, below,
beneath, beside, between,
(Slow)
beyond, but, by.

3. **Preposition, Preposition Starting with a D.**
down (slow & long),
during (snappy).

4. **Preposition, Preposition Don't go away.
Go to the middle
And see what we say.
E-F-I and L-N-O**
except, for, from,
in, inside, into,
like,
near, of, off,
on, out, outside, over.

5. **Preposition, Preposition Almost through.
Start with P and end with W.**
past, since, through,
throughout, to, toward,
under, underneath,
until, up, upon,
with, within, without.

6. **Preposition, Preposition Easy as can be.
We're all finished,
And aren't you pleased?
We've just recited
All 49 of these.**

Jingle 10: Pronoun Jingle

This little pronoun,
Floating around,
Takes the place of a little old noun.
With a knick knack, paddy wack,
These are English rules.
Isn't language fun and cool?

Jingle 11: Subject Pronoun Jingle

There are seven subject pronouns
That are easy as can be:
I and we,   (clap 2 times)
He and she,   (clap 2 times)
It and they and you.   (clap 3 times)

Jingle Section

Jingle 12: Possessive Pronoun Jingle

There are seven possessive pronouns
That are easy as can be:
My and our,   (clap 2 times)
His and her,   (clap 2 times)
Its and their and your. (clap 3 times)

Jingle 13: Object Pronoun Jingle

There are seven object pronouns
That are easy as can be:
Me and us,   (clap 2 times)
Him and her,   (clap 2 times)
It and them and you.   (clap 3 times)

Jingle 14: The 23 Helping Verbs of the Mean, Lean Verb Machine Jingle

These 23 helping verbs will be on my test.
I gotta remember them so I can do my best.
I'll start out with 8 and finish with 15;
Just call me the mean, lean verb machine.

There are 8 **be** verbs that are easy as can be:
  am, is, are – was and were,
  am, is, are – was and were,
  am, is, are – was and were,
  be, being, and been.

All together now, the 8 **be** verbs:
am, is, are – was and were – be, being, and been.
am, is, are – was and were – be, being, and been.

There're 23 helping verbs, and I've recited only 8.
That leaves fifteen more that I must relate:
  has, have, and had – do, does, and did,
  has, have, and had – do, does, and did,
  might, must, may – might, must, may.

Knowing these verbs will save my grade:
  can and could – would and should,
  can and could – would and should,
  shall and will,
  shall and will.

In record time, I did this drill.
I'm the mean, lean verb machine - STILL!

Jingle 15: Eight Parts of Speech Jingle

Want to know how to write?
Use the eight parts of speech - They're dynamite!

Nouns, **V**erbs, and **P**ronouns - They rule!
They're called the **NVP's**, and they're really cool!

The **Double A's** are on the move;
Adjectives and **A**dverbs help you groove!

Next come the **PIC's**, and then we're done!
The **PIC's** are **P**reposition, **I**nterjection, and **C**onjunction!

All together now, the eight parts of speech, abbreviations please:
NVP, AA, PIC   NVP, AA, PIC!

Jingle Section

Jingle 16: Direct Object Jingle

1. A direct object is a noun or pronoun.

2. A direct object completes the meaning of the sentence.

3. A direct object is located after the verb-transitive.

4. To find the direct object, ask WHAT or WHOM after your verb.

REFERENCE

SECTION

Vocabulary Reference – Level 3

Chapter 1, Vocabulary Words #1	Chapter 1, Vocabulary Words #2
(friendly, amiable, master, servant)	(small, minute, often, seldom)

Chapter 2, Vocabulary Words #1	Chapter 2, Vocabulary Words #2
(apt, suitable, certain, doubtful)	(clear, vague, tired, weary)

Chapter 3, Vocabulary Words #1	Chapter 3, Vocabulary Words #2
(kind, irreverent, curiosity, interest)	(bland, tasty, cut, sever)

Chapter 4, Vocabulary Words #1	Chapter 4, Vocabulary Words #2
(attempt, try, clean, soiled)	(column, pillar, eager, indifferent)

Chapter 5, Vocabulary Words #1	Chapter 5, Vocabulary Words #2
(watch, vigil, flabby, firm)	(cheap, costly, lethal, deadly)

Chapter 6, Vocabulary Words #1	Chapter 6, Vocabulary Words #2
(explode, burst, present, absent)	(send, receive, fowl, chicken)

Chapter 7, Vocabulary Words #1	Chapter 7, Vocabulary Words #2
(truthful, honest, congeal, melt)	(foe, friend, pain, discomfort)

Chapter 8, Vocabulary Words #1	Chapter 8, Vocabulary Words #2
(safe, endangered, unity, accord)	(tempt, lure, savage, tame)

Chapter 9, Vocabulary Words #1	Chapter 9, Vocabulary Words #2
(timid, bold, hurry, rush)	(fragrance, aroma, join, withdraw)

Chapter 10, Vocabulary Words #1	Chapter 10, Vocabulary Words #2
(abundant, scarce, wilt, droop)	(tepid, warm, frivolous, serious)

Chapter 11, Vocabulary Words #1	Chapter 11, Vocabulary Words #2
(intentional, unintended, annoy, aggravate)	(evade, avoid, oppose, support)

Vocabulary Reference – Level 3 (continued)

Chapter 12, Vocabulary Words #1	Chapter 12, Vocabulary Words #2
(stay, depart, victor, winner)	(fixed, repaired, gorgeous, unsightly)

Chapter 13, Vocabulary Words #1	Chapter 13, Vocabulary Words #2
(cover, wrap, courage, fear)	(famous, obscure, pleasure, joy)

Chapter 14, Vocabulary Words #1	Chapter 14, Vocabulary Words #2
(puny, robust, illness, disease)	(smart, intelligent, consistent, irregular)

Chapter 15, Vocabulary Words #1	Chapter 15, Vocabulary Words #2
(occupied, vacant, hidden, concealed)	(distant, remote, censor, permit)

Chapter 16, Vocabulary Words #1	Chapter 16, Vocabulary Words #2
(pretend, imagine, plentiful, sparse)	(sorrow, bliss, volunteer, offer)

Chapter 17, Vocabulary Words #1	Chapter 17, Vocabulary Words #2
(identical, alike, unprotected, guarded)	(tidy, cluttered, slope, incline)

Chapter 18, Vocabulary Words #1	Chapter 18, Vocabulary Words #2
(allow, thwart, unusual, strange)	(crevice, crack, defeat, victory)

Chapter 19, Vocabulary Words #1	Chapter 19, Vocabulary Words #2
(destroy, construct, insightful, perceptive)	(rejoice, celebrate, private, public)

Chapter 20, Vocabulary Words #1	Chapter 20, Vocabulary Words #2
(pause, hesitate, delete, insert)	(laborious, effortless, excuse, alibi)

Chapter 21, Vocabulary Words #1	Chapter 21, Vocabulary Words #2
(abrupt, sudden, torrid, frigid)	(link, disconnect, most, maximum)

Chapter 22, Vocabulary Words #1	Chapter 22, Vocabulary Words #2
(craze, fad, illiterate, educated)	(offend, compliment, wicked, evil)

State Information for the 50 States

Chapter	State	Capital	Postal Abbreviation	Admitted to Union
1. C 3	Alabama	Montgomery	AL	1819
2. C 4	Alaska	Juneau	AK	1959
3. C 5	Arizona	Phoenix	AZ	1912
4. C 6	Arkansas	Little Rock	AR	1836
5. C 7	California	Sacramento	CA	1850
6. C 7	Colorado	Denver	CO	1876
7. C 8	Connecticut	Hartford	CT	1788
8. C 8	Delaware	Dover	DE	1787
9. C 9	Florida	Tallahassee	FL	1845
10. C 9	Georgia	Atlanta	GA	1788
11. C 10	Hawaii	Honolulu	HI	1959
12. C 10	Idaho	Boise	ID	1890
13. C 11	Illinois	Springfield	IL	1818
14. C 11	Indiana	Indianapolis	IN	1816
15. C 12	Iowa	Des Moines	IA	1846
16. C 12	Kansas	Topeka	KS	1861
17. C 13	Kentucky	Frankfort	KY	1792
18. C 13	Louisiana	Baton Rouge	LA	1812
19. C 14	Maine	Augusta	ME	1820
20. C 14	Maryland	Annapolis	MD	1788
21. C 15	Massachusetts	Boston	MA	1788
22. C 15	Michigan	Lansing	MI	1837
23. C 16	Minnesota	St. Paul	MN	1858
24. C 16	Mississippi	Jackson	MS	1817
25. C 17	Missouri	Jefferson City	MO	1821
26. C 17	Montana	Helena	MT	1889
27. C 18	Nebraska	Lincoln	NE	1867
28. C 18	Nevada	Carson City	NV	1864
29. C 19	New Hampshire	Concord	NH	1788
30. C 19	New Jersey	Trenton	NJ	1787
31. C 20	New Mexico	Santa Fe	NM	1912
32. C 20	New York	Albany	NY	1788
33. C 21	North Carolina	Raleigh	NC	1789
34. C 21	North Dakota	Bismarck	ND	1889
35. C 22	Ohio	Columbus	OH	1803
36. C 22	Oklahoma	Oklahoma City	OK	1907
37. C 23	Oregon	Salem	OR	1859
38. C 23	Pennsylvania	Harrisburg	PA	1787
39. C 24	Rhode Island	Providence	RI	1790
40. C 24	South Carolina	Columbia	SC	1788
41. C 24	South Dakota	Pierre	SD	1889
42. C 24	Tennessee	Nashville	TN	1796
43. C 25	Texas	Austin	TX	1845
44. C 25	Utah	Salt Lake City	UT	1896
45. C 25	Vermont	Montpelier	VT	1791
46. C 25	Virginia	Richmond	VA	1788
47. C 25	Washington	Olympia	WA	1889
48. C 25	West Virginia	Charleston	WV	1863
49. C 25	Wisconsin	Madison	WI	1848
50. C 25	Wyoming	Cheyenne	WY	1890

Card Sample for State Information

1. What is the state on the front of this card? **Alabama**
2. What is the capital of Alabama? **Montgomery**
3. What is the postal abbreviation of Alabama? **AL**
4. What year was Alabama admitted to the Union? **1819**

Reference 1: Beginning Setup Plan for Homeschool

You should use this plan to keep things in order!

1. Have separate color-coded pocket folders for each subject.
2. Put unfinished work in the right-hand side and finished work in the left-hand side of each subject folder.
3. Put notes to study, graded tests, and study guides in the brads so you will have them to study for scheduled tests.
4. Have a paper folder to store extra clean sheets of paper. Keep it full at all times.
5. Have an assignment folder to be reviewed every day.

Things to keep in your assignment folder:

A. Keep a monthly calendar of assignments, test dates, report-due dates, project-due dates, extra activities, dates and times, review dates, etc.

B. Keep a grade sheet to record the grades received in each subject.

   (*You might also consider keeping your grades on the inside cover of each subject folder. However you keep your grades, just remember to record them accurately. Your grades are your business, so keep up with them! Grades help you know which areas need attention.*)

C. Make a list every day of the things you want to do so you can keep track of what you finish and what you have not finished. Move the unfinished items to your new list the next day.

   (*Making this list takes time, but it's your road map to success. You will always know at a glance what you set out to accomplish and what still needs to be done.*)

6. Keep all necessary school supplies in a handy, heavy-duty Ziploc bag or a pencil bag.

Reference 2: What is Journal Writing?

Journal Writing is a written record of your personal thoughts and feelings about things or people that are important to you. Recording your thoughts in a journal is a good way to remember how you felt about what was happening in your life at a particular time. You can record your dreams, memories, feelings, and experiences. You can ask questions and answer some of them. It is fun to go back later and read what you have written because it shows how you have changed in different areas of your life. A journal can also be an excellent place to look for future writing topics, creative stories, poems, etc. Writing in a journal is an easy and enjoyable way to practice your writing skills without worrying about a writing grade.

What do I write about?

Journals are personal, but sometimes it helps to have ideas to get you started. Remember, in a journal, you do not have to stick to one topic. Write about someone or something you like. Write about what you did last weekend or on vacation. Write about what you hope to do this week or on your next vacation. Write about home, school, friends, hobbies, special talents *(yours or someone else's),* or present and future hopes and fears. Write about what is wrong in your world and what you would do to "fix" it. Write about the good things and the bad things in your world.

If you think about a past event and want to write an opinion about it now, put it in your journal. If you want to give your opinion about a present or future event that could have an impact on your life or the way that you see things, put it in your journal. If something bothers you, record it in your journal. If something interests you, record it. If you just want to record something that doesn't seem important at all, write it in your journal. After all, it is your journal!

How do I get started writing in my personal journal?

You need to put the day's date on the title line of your paper: **Month, Day, Year.** Skip the next line and begin your entry. You might write one or two sentences, a paragraph, a whole page, or several pages. Except for the journal date, no particular organizational style is required for journal writing. You decide how best to organize and express your thoughts. Feel free to include sketches, diagrams, lists, etc., if they will help you remember your thoughts about a topic or an event. You will also need a spiral notebook, a pen, a quiet place, and at least 5-10 minutes of uninterrupted writing time.

Note: Use a pen if possible. Pencils have erasers and lead points that break, both of which slow down your thoughts. Any drawings you might include do not have to be masterpieces—stick figures will do nicely.

Reference 3: Synonyms, Antonyms, and Five-Step Vocabulary Plan

Part 1: Synonyms and Antonyms

Definitions: Synonyms are words that have similar, or almost the same, meanings.
Antonyms are words that have opposite meanings.

Directions: Identify each pair of words as synonyms or antonyms by putting parentheses ( ) around **syn** or **ant**.

| 1. noisy, loud | **(syn)** ant | 2. damp, wet | **(syn)** ant | 3. add, subtract | syn **(ant)** |

Part 2: Five-Step Vocabulary Plan

(1) Write a title for the vocabulary words in each chapter.
   Example: Chapter 1, Vocabulary Words

(2) Write each vocabulary word in your vocabulary notebook.

(3) Look up each vocabulary word in a dictionary or thesaurus.

(4) Write the meaning beside each vocabulary word.

(5) Write a sentence that helps you remember how each vocabulary word is used.

Reference 4: A and An Choices

Rule 1: Use the word **a** when the next word begins with a consonant sound. (*Example: a hairy ape.*)
Rule 2: Use the word **an** when the next word begins with a vowel sound. (*Example: an ape.*)

Example Sentences: Write **a** or **an** in the blanks.

1. They moved into ___**an**___ apartment.

2. They moved into ___**a**___ new apartment.

3. She noticed ___**a**___ change in his attitude.

4. She noticed ___**an**___ obvious change in his attitude.

Reference 5: My Sentence Book Series, Book 1

Part A	Part B
My **Sentence Book** **Series** **Book #1** **By:** (*Write your name.*) **Date:** (*Write the date.*)	Page 1: Horse runs. Page 2: Horse jumps. Page 3: Horse walks. Page 4: Horse eats. Page 5: Horse sleeps. Page 6: The End.

Reference 6: My Sentence Book Series, Book 2

Part A	Part B
My **Sentence Book** **Series** **Book #2** **By:** (*Write your name.*) **Date:** (*Write the date.*)	Page 1: Horse runs fast. Page 2: Horse jumps high. Page 3: Horse walks slowly. Page 4: Horse eats quickly. Page 5: Horse sleeps soundly. Page 6: The End.

Reference 7: My Sentence Book Series, Book 3

Part A	Part B
My **Sentence Book** **Series** **Book #3** **By:** (*Write your name.*) **Date:** (*Write the date.*)	Page 1: The beautiful horse runs fast. Page 2: The excited young horse jumps very high. Page 3: An old horse walks slowly away. Page 4: The hungry horse eats quickly. Page 5: The tired horse sleeps soundly. Page 6: The End.

Reference 8: Question and Answer Flow Sentence

Question and Answer Flow Sentence: The happy young man whistled cheerfully.

1. Who whistled cheerfully? man - SN
2. What is being said about man? man whistled - V
3. Whistled how? cheerfully - Adv
4. What kind of man? young - Adj
5. What kind of man? happy - Adj
6. The - A

Classified Sentence:

A	Adj	Adj	SN	V	Adv
The	happy	young	man	whistled	cheerfully.

Reference 9: Additional Article Adjective Information

The article *The* has two pronunciations:

a. As a long **e** (*where the article comes in front of a word that begins with a vowel sound*)
   the egg, the igloo, the excellent meal

b. As a short **u** (*where the article comes in front of a word that begins with a consonant sound*)
   the dance, the shoe, the green trees

Reference 10: The Four Kinds of Sentences and the End Mark Flow

1. A **declarative** sentence makes a statement. It is labeled with a **D**.
Example: Jane ran every morning.
(Period, statement, declarative sentence)

2. An **imperative** sentence gives a command. It is labeled with an **Imp**.
Example: Take the students to class.
(Period, command, imperative sentence)

3. An **interrogative** sentence asks a question. It is labeled with an **Int**.
Example: How many books did you read?
(Question mark, question, interrogative sentence)

4. An **exclamatory** sentence expresses strong feeling. It is labeled with an **E**.
Example: The alligator snapped at us!
(Exclamation point, strong feeling, exclamatory sentence)

Examples: Read each sentence, recite the end-mark flow in parentheses, and put the end mark and the abbreviation for the sentence type in the blank at the end of each sentence.

1. My dentist is a nice man **. D**
(Period, statement, declarative sentence)

2. The strong wind shook our windows **! E**
(Exclamation point, strong feeling, exclamatory sentence)

3. Take this medicine before noon **. Imp**
(Period, command, imperative sentence)

4. Will you come to our party tonight **? Int**
(Question mark, question, interrogative sentence)

Reference 11: Question and Answer Flow Sentence

Question and Answer Flow: The three spirited horses ran quickly away.

1. What ran quickly away? horses - SN
2. What is being said about horses? horses ran - V
3. Ran how? quickly - Adv
4. Ran where? away - Adv
5. What kind of horses? spirited - Adj
6. How many horses? three - Adj
7. The - A
8. SN V P1 Check
9. Period, statement, declarative sentence
10. Go back to the verb - divide the complete subject from the complete predicate.

Classified Sentence:

$$\underline{\text{SN V}} \quad \begin{array}{ccccccc} \text{A} & \text{Adj} & \text{Adj} & \text{SN} & \text{V} & \text{Adv} & \text{Adv} \\ \end{array}$$
SN V   The three spirited horses / ran quickly away. **D**
P1

Reference 12: Definitions for a Skill Builder Check

1. A **noun** names a person, place, or thing.

2. A **singular noun** usually does not end in *s* or *es* and means only one. (*ring, cloud, star*)
   Exception: Some nouns that end in s are singular and mean only one. (*mattress, bus*)

3. A **plural noun** usually ends in *s* or *es* and means more than one. (*rings, clouds, stars*)
   Exception: Some nouns are made plural by changing their spelling. (*goose-geese, child-children*)

4. A **common noun** names ANY person, place, or thing. A common noun is not capitalized because it does not name a specific person, place, or thing. (*doctor, park*)

5. A **proper noun** is a noun that names a specific, or particular, person, place, or thing. Proper nouns are always capitalized no matter where they are located in the sentence. (*James, New York*)

6. A **simple subject** is another name for the subject noun or subject pronoun.

7. A **simple predicate** is another name for the verb.

Reference 13: Checklists
Revision Checklist

1. Eliminate unnecessary or needlessly-repeated words or ideas.
2. Combine or reorder sentences.
3. Change word choices for clarity and expression.
4. Know the purpose: to explain, to describe, to entertain, or to persuade.
5. Know the audience: the reader(s) of the writing.

Beginning Editing Checklist

1. Did you indent the paragraph?
2. Did you capitalize the first word and put an end mark at the end of every sentence?
3. Did you spell words correctly?

More Editing Skills

4. Did you follow the writing guidelines? (*located in Reference 19 on student page 20*)
5. Did you list the topic and two points (or three points) on separate lines at the top of the paper?
6. Did you follow the two-point (or three-point) paragraph pattern?
7. Did you use the correct homonyms?
8. Did you follow all other capitalization and punctuation rules?
9. Did you follow the three-paragraph essay pattern?

Final Paper Checklist

1. Have you written the correct heading on your paper?
2. Have you written your final paper in ink?
3. Have you single-spaced your final paper?
4. Have you written your final paper neatly?
5. Have you stapled the final paper to the rough draft and handed them in to your teacher?

Writing Process Checklist

1. Gather information.
2. Write a rough draft.
3. Revise the rough draft.
4. Edit the rough draft.
5. Write a final paper.

Reference 14: Drafts and Final Paragraph

Rough Draft

Before Dustin left for work, he shut Harvey his new puppy in the laundry room. Harvey whimpered wined and scratched at the door. Dustin ignored Harvey as he quickly headed out the door. On his lunch brake, he came back home to check on harvey. When he opened the laundry room door Harvey bolted out and ran through the house. Dustin looked at the big mess the puppy had made. Harvey had turned over his food and water bowl. Wet newspapers were shredded and spread all over the floor. Dustin sighed and began to clean up Harveys mess. Before he finished, Dustin heard a crash in the kitchen. Harvey had turned over the trashcan

Revision of Draft

Before Dustin left for work, he shut Harvey his new puppy in the laundry room. Harvey whimpered wined and scratched at the door. Dustin ignored **Harveys complaint as he rushed** out the door. On his lunch brake, he came back home to check on harvey. When he opened the laundry room door Harvey bolted out and **dashed** through the house. Dustin **stared** at the **huge** mess the puppy had made. Harvey had turned over his food and water bowl. Wet newspapers were shredded and **scattered** all over the floor. Dustin sighed **as he** began to clean up Harveys mess. Before **Dustin** finished, **he** heard a crash in the kitchen. Harvey had turned over the trashcan

Edit Draft

Before Dustin left for work, he shut Harvey, **[comma inserted]** his new puppy, **[comma inserted]** in the laundry room. Harvey whimpered, **[comma inserted]** whined, **[comma inserted]** and scratched at the door. Dustin ignored Harvey's **[apostrophe added]** complaint as he rushed out the door. On his lunch **break, [*break,* not *brake*]** he came back home to check on **Harvey [*Harvey,* not *harvey*]**. When he opened the laundry room door, **[comma inserted]** Harvey bolted out and dashed through the house. Dustin stared at the huge mess the puppy had made. Harvey had turned over his food and water bowl. Wet newspapers were shredded and scattered all over the floor. Dustin sighed as he began to clean up Harvey's **[apostrophe added]** mess. Before he finished, Dustin heard a crash in the kitchen. Harvey had turned over the trashcan! **[End mark]**

Final Paragraph

Before Dustin left for work, he shut Harvey, his new puppy, in the laundry room. Harvey whimpered, whined, and scratched at the door. Dustin ignored Harvey's complaint as he rushed out the door. On his lunch break, he came back home to check on Harvey. When he opened the laundry room door, Harvey bolted out and dashed through the house. Dustin stared at the huge mess the puppy had made. Harvey had turned over his food and water bowl. Wet newspapers were shredded and scattered all over the floor. Dustin sighed as he began to clean up Harvey's mess. Before he finished, Dustin heard a crash in the kitchen. Harvey had turned over the trashcan!

Reference 15: Noun Job Chart

Directions: Classify the sentence below. Underline the complete subject once and the complete predicate twice. Then, complete the table.

```
                   A      Adj     SN       V       Adv      Adv
1. SN  V           The bewildered  hikers / stumbled desperately forward.  D
   P1
```

List the Noun Used	List the Noun Job	Singular or Plural	Common or Proper	Simple Subject	Simple Predicate
hikers	SN	P	C	hikers	stumbled

Reference 16: Practice Sentence

Labels:	A	Adj	Adj	SN	V	Adv	Adv
Practice:	**The**	**shy**	**young**	**lady**	**spoke**	**very**	**softly.**

Reference 17: Improved Sentence

Labels:	A	Adj	Adj	SN	V	Adv	Adv
Practice:	The	shy	young	lady	spoke	very	softly.
Improved:	**A**	**reserved**	**elderly**	**woman**	**chatted**	**quite**	**earnestly.**
	(word change)	(synonym)	(antonym)	(synonym)	(synonym)	(synonym)	(word change)

Reference 18: Two-Point Paragraph Example

Topic: **My favorite colors**
Two main points: 1. **green** 2. **yellow**

Sentence #1 – <u>Topic Sentence</u> (*Use words in the topic and tell how many points will be used.*)
I have two favorite colors.

Sentence #2 – <u>2-Point Sentence</u> (*List the 2 points in the order you will present them.*)
These colors are green and yellow.

Sentence #3 – <u>First Point</u>
My first favorite color is green.

Sentence #4 – <u>Supporting Sentence</u> for the first point.
I like green because I love budding leaves after a long winter.

Sentence #5 – <u>Second Point</u>
My second favorite color is yellow.

Sentence #6 – <u>Supporting Sentence</u> for the second point.
Yellow reminds me of warm sunshine and summer days.

Sentence #7 – <u>Concluding (final) Sentence</u> (*Restate the topic sentence and add an extra thought.*)
My two favorite colors remind me of summer, which has an abundance of green and yellow everywhere.

<u>SAMPLE PARAGRAPH</u>

My Favorite Colors

I have two favorite colors. These colors are green and yellow. My first favorite color is green. I like green because I love budding leaves after a long winter. My second favorite color is yellow. Yellow reminds me of warm sunshine and summer days. My two favorite colors remind me of summer, which has an abundance of green and yellow everywhere.

Reference 19: Writing Guidelines

1. Label your writing assignment in the top right-hand corner of your page with the following information:

   A. Your Name
   B. The Writing Assignment Number. *(Examples: WA#1, WA#2, etc.)*
   C. Type of Writing *(Examples: Expository Paragraph, Persuasive Essay, Descriptive Paragraph, etc.)*
   D. The title of the writing on the top of the first line.

2. Think about the topic that you are assigned.

3. Think about the type of writing assigned, which is the purpose for the writing.
   (Is your writing intended to explain, persuade, describe, or narrate?)

4. Think about the writing format, which is the organizational plan you are expected to use.
   (Is your assignment a paragraph, a 3-paragraph essay, or a letter?)

5. Use your writing time wisely.
   (Begin work quickly and concentrate on your assignment until it is finished.)

Reference 20: Knowing the Difference Between Prepositions and Adverbs

Adv
In the sample sentence, *Alexander fell **down***, the word ***down*** is an adverb because it does not have a noun after it.

P   noun (OP)
In the sample sentence, *Alexander fell **down the steps***, the word ***down*** is a preposition because it has the noun ***steps*** (the object of the preposition) after it. To find the preposition and object of the preposition in the Question and Answer Flow, say:

down – P (Say: *down – preposition*)
down what? steps – OP (Say: *down what? steps – object of the preposition*)

Reference 21: Subject-Verb Agreement Rules

Rule 1: A singular subject must use a singular verb form that ends in **s**: *is, was, has, does,* or *verbs ending with* **es**.
Rule 2: A plural subject, a compound subject, or the subject **YOU** must use a plural verb form that has **no s** ending: *are, were, do, have,* or *verbs without* **s** *or* **es** *endings*. (A plural verb form is also called the *plain form*.)

Examples: For each sentence, do these four things: (1) Write the subject. (2) Write **S** if the subject is singular or **P** if the subject is plural. (3) Write the rule number. (4) Underline the correct verb in the sentence.

Subject	S or P	Rule	
clock	S	1	1. The cuckoo **clock** (<u>chimes</u>, chime) on the hour.
rosebush and lilacs	P	2	2. The **rosebush** and the **lilacs** (<u>were</u>, was) blooming beautifully.
You	P	2	3. **You** (waits, <u>wait</u>) until we have gone.

Reference 22: Subject Pronoun

1. A **subject pronoun** takes the place of a noun that is used as the subject of a sentence.
2. These are the most common subject pronouns: *I, we, he, she, it, they*, and *you*. Use the Subject Pronoun Jingle to remember the common subject pronouns.
3. To find a subject pronoun, ask the subject question *who* or *what*.
4. Label a subject pronoun with an *SP*.
5. Call the **SP** abbreviation a subject pronoun.

Reference 23: Understood Subject Pronoun

1. A sentence has an **understood subject** when someone gives a command or makes a request and leaves the subject unwritten or unspoken. It is understood that the unspoken subject will always be the pronoun *you*.
2. An imperative sentence gives a command or makes a request. It ends with a period or an exclamation point and always has the word *you* understood, but not expressed, as the subject.
3. The understood subject pronoun *you* is always written in parentheses at the beginning of the sentence with the label *SP* beside or above it: **(You) SP**.
4. Call the abbreviation **(You) SP** an understood subject pronoun.

Reference 24: Possessive Pronouns

1. A possessive pronoun takes the place of a possessive noun.
2. A possessive pronoun's spelling form makes it possessive. These are the most common possessive pronouns: *my, our, his, her, its, their*, and *your*. Use the Possessive Pronoun Jingle to remember the most common possessive pronouns.
3. A possessive pronoun has two jobs: to show ownership or possession and to modify like an adjective.
4. When classifying a possessive pronoun, both jobs will be recognized by labeling the pronoun as a possessive pronoun adjective. Use the abbreviation **PPA** (possessive pronoun adjective).
5. Include possessive pronouns when you are asked to identify pronouns, possessives, or adjectives.
6. To find a possessive pronoun, begin with the question *whose*. (*Whose medicine? His - PPA*)

Reference 25: Object Pronoun

1. If a pronoun does any job that has the word *object* in it, that pronoun is an object pronoun. Object pronouns can be used as objects of the prepositions, direct objects, or indirect objects.

2. The object pronouns are listed in your Object Pronoun Jingle: *me, us, him, her, it, them,* and *you.*

3. An object pronoun does not have a special label. An object pronoun keeps the **OP**, **DO**, or **IO** label that tells its job.

	OP	DO	IO
Examples:	My dad played with *us.*	The boss called *him.*	Send *her* a message.

Reference 26: Singular and Plural Points

Two-Point Expository Paragraph

Topic: My favorite fruits

2-points: 1. peaches 2. pineapples

     I have two favorite fruits. These fruits are peaches and pineapples. My first favorite fruit is a peach. I like peaches because they are so refreshing and sweet. My second favorite fruit is a pineapple. I love the tropical flavor of ice-cold pineapples. I enjoy eating all kinds of fruits, but my favorites will always be peaches and pineapples.

Reference 27: Possessive Nouns

1. A possessive noun is the name of a person, place, or thing that owns something.

2. A possessive noun will always have an apostrophe after it. It will be either an *apostrophe s ('s)* or an *s apostrophe (s')*. The apostrophe makes a noun show ownership. (*Linda's car*)

3. A possessive noun has two jobs: to show ownership or possession and to modify like an adjective.

4. When classifying a possessive noun, both jobs will be recognized by labeling it as a possessive noun adjective. Use the abbreviation **PNA** (possessive noun adjective).

5. Include possessive nouns when you are asked to identify possessive nouns or adjectives. Do not include possessive nouns when you are asked to identify regular nouns.

6. To find a possessive noun, begin with the question *whose.* (*Whose car? Linda's - PNA*)

Reference 28: Making Nouns Possessive

1. For a singular noun - add ('s)	2. For a plural noun that ends in *s* - add (')	3. For a plural noun that does not end in *s* - add ('s)
Rule 1: girl's	**Rule 2: girls'**	**Rule 3: women's**

Part A: Underline each noun to be made possessive and write singular or plural (**S-P**), the rule number, and the possessive form. Part B: Write each noun as singular possessive and then as plural possessive.

Part A	S-P	Rule	Possessive Form	Part B	Singular Poss	Plural Poss
1. <u>carpenter</u> saw	S	1	carpenter's saw	5. knife	**knife's**	**knives'**
2. <u>lawyers</u> clients	P	2	lawyers' clients	6. plane	**plane's**	**planes'**
3. <u>Frank</u> address	S	1	Frank's address	7. scientist	**scientist's**	**scientists'**
4. <u>animal</u> dens	S	1	animal's dens	8. boy	**boy's**	**boys'**

Reference 29: Two- and Three-Point Expository Paragraph Guidelines

2-Point Expository Paragraph Guidelines Paragraph (7 sentences)

A. Topic sentence

B. A two-point sentence

C. A **first-point sentence**

D. A **supporting** sentence for the first point

E. A **second-point sentence**

F. A **supporting** sentence for the second point

G. A concluding sentence

3-Point Expository Paragraph Guidelines Paragraph (9 sentences)

A. Topic sentence

B. A three-point sentence

C. A **first-point sentence**

D. A **supporting** sentence for the first point

E. A **second-point sentence**

F. A **supporting** sentence for the second point

G. A **third-point sentence**

H. A **supporting** sentence for the third point

I. A concluding sentence

Reference 30: Three-Point Expository Paragraph Example

Topic: **My favorite colors**
Three main points: 1. **green**   2. **yellow**   3. **red**

Sentence #1 – <u>Topic Sentence</u> (*Use words in the topic and tell how many points will be used.*)
I have three favorite colors.

Sentence #2 – <u>3-Point Sentence</u> (*List the 3 points in the order you will present them.*)
These colors are green, yellow, and red.

Sentence #3 – <u>First Point</u>
My first favorite color is green.

Sentence #4 – <u>Supporting Sentence</u> for the first point.
I like green because I love budding leaves after a long winter.

Sentence #5 – <u>Second Point</u>
My second favorite color is yellow.

Sentence #6 – <u>Supporting Sentence</u> for the second point.
Yellow reminds me of warm sunshine and summer days.

Sentence #7 – <u>Third Point</u>
My third favorite color is red.

Sentence #8 – <u>Supporting Sentence</u> for the third point.
Red is a wonderful, rich color for celebrating winter holidays.

Sentence #9 – <u>Concluding (final) Sentence</u>. (*Restate the topic sentence and add an extra thought.*)
My three favorite colors remind me of special seasons throughout the year.

SAMPLE PARAGRAPH

My Favorite Colors

I have three favorite colors. These colors are green, yellow, and red. My first favorite color is green. I like green because I love budding leaves after a long winter. My second favorite color is yellow. Yellow reminds me of warm sunshine and summer days. My third favorite color is red. Red is a wonderful, rich color for celebrating winter holidays. My three favorite colors remind me of special seasons throughout the year.

General Checklist: Check the Finished Paragraph	The Three-Point Expository Paragraph Outline
(1) Have you followed the pattern for a 3-point paragraph? (*Indent, topic sentence, 3-point sentence, 3 main points, 3 supporting sentences, and a concluding sentence.*)	Topic 3 points about the topic Sentence #1: **Topic** sentence Sentence #2: A **three-point** sentence
(2) Do you have complete sentences?	Sentence #3: A **first-point sentence**
(3) Have you capitalized the first word and put an end mark at the end of every sentence?	Sentence #4: A **supporting** sentence for the 1st point
(4) Have you checked your sentences for capitalization and punctuation mistakes?	Sentence #5: A **second-point sentence** Sentence #6: A **supporting** sentence for the 2nd point
(5) Have you checked your verb tenses?	Sentence #7: A **third-point sentence**
(6) Have you varied your sentence structure?	Sentence #8: A **supporting** sentence for the 3rd point Sentence #9: A **concluding** sentence

Reference 31: Irregular Verb Chart

PRESENT	PAST	PAST PARTICIPLE		PRESENT PARTICIPLE	
become	became	(has)	become	(is)	becoming
blow	blew	(has)	blown	(is)	blowing
break	broke	(has)	broken	(is)	breaking
bring	brought	(has)	brought	(is)	bringing
burst	burst	(has)	burst	(is)	bursting
buy	bought	(has)	bought	(is)	buying
choose	chose	(has)	chosen	(is)	choosing
come	came	(has)	come	(is)	coming
drink	drank	(has)	drunk	(is)	drinking
drive	drove	(has)	driven	(is)	driving
eat	ate	(has)	eaten	(is)	eating
fall	fell	(has)	fallen	(is)	falling
fly	flew	(has)	flown	(is)	flying
freeze	froze	(has)	frozen	(is)	freezing
get	got	(has)	gotten	(is)	getting
give	gave	(has)	given	(is)	giving
grow	grew	(has)	grown	(is)	growing
know	knew	(has)	known	(is)	knowing
lie	lay	(has)	lain	(is)	lying
lay	laid	(has)	laid	(is)	laying
make	made	(has)	made	(is)	making
ride	rode	(has)	ridden	(is)	riding
ring	rang	(has)	rung	(is)	ringing
rise	rose	(has)	risen	(is)	rising
sell	sold	(has)	sold	(is)	selling
sing	sang	(has)	sung	(is)	singing
sink	sank	(has)	sunk	(is)	sinking
set	set	(has)	set	(is)	setting
sit	sat	(has)	sat	(is)	sitting
shoot	shot	(has)	shot	(is)	shooting
swim	swam	(has)	swum	(is)	swimming
take	took	(has)	taken	(is)	taking
tell	told	(has)	told	(is)	telling
throw	threw	(has)	thrown	(is)	throwing
wear	wore	(has)	worn	(is)	wearing
write	wrote	(has)	written	(is)	writing

Reference 32: Paragraphs Using Different Writing Forms

Topic: My favorite collectibles **3-points:** 1. stuffed animals   2. sea shells   3. rocks

Example 1: Three-point paragraph using time-order points

     I have three favorite collectibles. They are stuffed animals, sea shells, and rocks. **First**, I like to collect stuffed animals. Stuffed animals are so cuddly and adorable. **Second**, I like to collect sea shells. It is fun collecting seashells while I walk along the beach and wade in the water. **Third**, I like to collect rocks. (or **Finally**, *I like to collect rocks.*) Since rocks can be found in so many different sizes, shapes, and colors, I use them to make a memory garden. I enjoy collecting many things, but collecting stuffed animals, sea shells, and rocks holds a special fascination for me.

Example 2: Three-point paragraph using a standard topic sentence with different time-order points

     I have three favorite collectibles. They are stuffed animals, sea shells, and rocks. **First**, I like to collect stuffed animals. Stuffed animals are so cuddly and adorable. **Next**, I like to collect sea shells. It is fun collecting seashells while I walk along the beach and wade in the water. **Last**, I like to collect rocks. (or **Finally**, *I like to collect rocks.*) Since rocks can be found in so many different sizes, shapes, and colors, I use them to make a memory garden. I enjoy collecting many things, but collecting stuffed animals, sea shells, and rocks holds a special fascination for me.

Reference 33: Homonym Chart

Homonyms are words that sound the same but have different meanings and different spellings.

1. **capital** - upper part, main	15. **lead** - metal	29. **their** - belonging to them
2. **capitol** - statehouse	16. **led** - guided	30. **there** - in that place
3. **coarse** - rough	17. **no** - not so	31. **they're** - they are
4. **course** - route	18. **know** - to understand	32. **threw** - did throw
5. **council** - assembly	19. **right** - correct	33. **through** - from end to end
6. **counsel** - advice	20. **write** - to form letters	34. **to** - toward, preposition
7. **forth** - forward	21. **principle** - a truth/rule/law	35. **too** - denoting excess
8. **fourth** - ordinal number	22. **principal** - chief/head person	36. **two** - a couple
9. **its** - possessive pronoun	23. **stationary** - motionless	37. **your** - belonging to you
10. **it's** - it is	24. **stationery** - paper	38. **you're** - you are
11. **hear** - to listen	25. **peace** - quiet	39. **weak** - not strong
12. **here** - in this place	26. **piece** - a part	40. **week** - seven days
13. **knew** - understood	27. **sent** - caused to go	41. **days** - more than one day
14. **new** - not old	28. **scent** - odor	42. **daze** - a confused state

Directions: Underline the correct homonym.

1. One (weak, **week**) has passed, and Sally hasn't called.
2. James felt (**weak**, week) after his knee surgery.

Reference 34: Capitalization Rules

SECTION 1: CAPITALIZE THE FIRST WORD

1. The first word of a sentence. (*He likes to take a nap.*)

2. The first word in the greeting and closing of letters. (*Dear, Yours truly*)

3. The first and last word and important words in titles of literary works.
   (*books, songs, short stories, poems, articles, movie titles, magazines*)
   (*Note: Conjunctions, articles, and prepositions with fewer than five letters are not capitalized unless they are the first or last word.*)

4. The first word of a direct quotation. (*Dad said, "We are going home."*)

5. The first word in each line of a topic outline.

SECTION 2: CAPITALIZE NAMES, INITIALS, AND TITLES OF PEOPLE

6. The pronoun I. (*May I go with you?*)

7. The names and nicknames of people. (*Sam, Joe, Jones, Slim, Shorty*)

8. Family names when used in place of or with the person's name.
   (*Grandmother, Auntie, Uncle Joe, Mother – Do NOT capitalize* my mother.)

9. Titles used with, or in place of, people's names.
   (*Mr., Ms., Miss, Dr. Smith, Doctor, Captain, President, Sir*)

10. People's initials. (*J. D., C. Smith*)

SECTION 3: CAPITALIZE WORDS OF TIME

11. The days of the week and months of the year. (*Monday, July*)

12. The names of holidays. (*Christmas, Thanksgiving, Easter*)

13. The names of historical events, periods, laws, documents, conflicts, and distinguished awards. (*Civil War, Middle Ages, Medal of Honor*)

SECTION 4: CAPITALIZE NAMES OF PLACES

14. The names and abbreviations of cities, towns, counties, states, countries, and nations.
    (*Dallas, Texas, Fulton County, Africa, America, USA, AR, TX*)

15. The names of avenues, streets, roads, highways, routes, and post office boxes.
    (*Main Street, Jones Road, Highway 89, Rt. 1, Box 2, P.O. Box 45*)

16. The names of lakes, rivers, oceans, mountain ranges, deserts, parks, stars, planets, and constellations.
    (*Beaver Lake, Rocky Mountains, Venus*)

17. The names of schools and titles of school courses that are numbered or are languages.
    (*Walker Elementary School, Mathematics II*)

18. North, south, east, and west when they refer to sections of the country.
    (*up North, live in the East, out West*)

SECTION 5: CAPITALIZE NAMES OF OTHER NOUNS AND PROPER ADJECTIVES

19. The names of pets. (*Spot, Tweety Bird, etc.*)

20. The names of products. (*Campbell's soup, Kelly's chili, Ford cars, etc.*)

21. The names of companies, buildings, ships, planes, space ships.
    (*Empire State Building, Titanic, IBM, The Big Tire Co.*)

22. Proper adjectives. (*the English language, Italian restaurant, French test*)

23. The names of clubs, organizations, or groups. (*Lion's Club, Jaycees, Beatles*)

24. The names of political parties, religious preferences, nationalities, and races.
    (*Democratic party, Republican, Jewish synagogue, American*)

Reference 35: Sentence Parts That Can Be Used for a Pattern 1 Sentence

1. **Nouns**

   Use *only* subject nouns or object of the preposition nouns.

2. **Adverbs**

   Tell how, when, or where.
   Can be placed before or after verbs, at the beginning or end of a sentence, and in front of adjectives or other adverbs.

3. **Adjectives**

   Tell what kind, which one, or how many.
   Can be placed in front of nouns. Sometimes, two or three adjectives can modify the same noun.

   Articles

   Adjectives that are used in front of nouns (a, an, the).

4. **Verbs** *(Can include helping verbs.)*

5. **Prepositional Phrases**

   Can be placed before or after nouns, after verbs, adverbs, or other prepositional phrases, and at the beginning or end of a sentence.

6. **Pronouns**

   (subjective, possessive, or objective)

7. **Conjunctions**

   Connecting words for compound parts: and, or, but.

8. **Interjections**

   Usually found at the beginning of a sentence. Can show strong or mild emotion.

Reference 36A: This reference is located on page 29.

Reference 36B: This reference is located on page 30.

Reference 37: Capitalization and Punctuation Examples

    1 6   9 7   3   3

1. **No, I** did not see the article **Mr. M**elbourne wrote for the popular magazine called <u>P</u>opular <u>S</u>cience**.**

    10   16   22   1

Editing Guide for Sample 1 Sentence: Capitals: 6   Periods: 1   Commas: 1   Underlining: 1   End Marks: 1

    Y   D   A

2. yes**,** donald**,** my brother**'**s boss**,** is australian**.**

Editing Guide for Sample 2 Sentence: Capitals: 3   Commas: 3   Apostrophes: 1   End Marks: 1

Reference 36A: Punctuation Rules

SECTION 1: END MARK PUNCTUATION

1. Use a (.) for the end punctuation of a sentence that makes a statement.
   (*Mom baked us a cake.*)
2. Use a (?) for the end punctuation of a sentence that asks a question.
   (*Are you going to town*?)
3. Use an (!) for the end punctuation of a sentence that expresses strong feeling.
   (*That bee stung me*!)
4. Use a (.) for the end punctuation of a sentence that gives a command or makes a request.
   (*Close the door.*)

SECTION 2: COMMAS TO SEPARATE TIME WORDS

5. Use a comma between the day of the week and the month. (*Friday, July 23*)
   Use a comma between the day and year. (*July 23, 2009*)
6. Use a comma to separate the year from the rest of the sentence when the year follows the month or the month and the day.
   (*We spent May, 2001, with Mom. We spent July 23, 2001, with Dad.*)

SECTION 3: COMMAS TO SEPARATE PLACE WORDS

7. Use a comma to separate the city from the state or country.
   (*I will go to Dallas, Texas. He is from Paris, France.*)
8. Use a comma to separate the state or country from the rest of the sentence when the name of the state or country follows the name of a city.
   (*We flew to Dallas, Texas, in June. We flew to Paris, France, in July.*)

SECTION 4: COMMAS TO MAKE MEANINGS CLEAR

9. Use a comma to separate words or phrases in a series.
   (*We had soup, crackers, and milk.*)
10. Use commas to separate introductory words such as *Yes, Well, Oh,* and *No* from the rest of a sentence.
    (*Oh, I didn't know that.*)
11. Use commas to set off most appositives. An appositive is a word, phrase, title, or degree used directly after another word or name to rename it.
    (*Sue, the girl next door, likes to draw.*)

    One-word appositives can be written two different ways: (1) *My brother, Tim, is riding in the horse show.* (2) *My brother Tim is riding in the horse show.* Your assignments will require one-word appositives to be set off with commas.
12. Use commas to separate a noun of direct address (the name of a person directly spoken to) from the rest of the sentence.
    (*Mom, do I really have to go?*)

SECTION 5: PUNCTUATION IN GREETINGS AND CLOSINGS OF LETTERS

13. Use a comma (,) after the salutation (greeting) of a friendly letter. (*Dear Sam,*)
14. Use a comma (,) after the closing of any letter. (*Yours truly,*)
15. Use a colon (:) after the salutation (greeting) of a business letter. (*Dear Madam:*)

Reference 36B: Punctuation Rules

SECTION 6: PERIODS

16. Use a period after most abbreviations or titles that are accepted in formal writing. (*Mr., Ms., Dr., Capt., St., Ave., St. Louis*) (*Note: These abbreviations cannot be used by themselves. They must always be used with a proper noun.*)

   In the abbreviations of many well-known organizations or words, periods are not required. (*USA, GM, TWA, GTE, AT&T, TV, AM, FM, GI, etc.*) Use only one period after an abbreviation at the end of a statement. Do not put an extra period for the end mark punctuation.

17. Use a period after initials. (*C. Smith, D.J. Brewton, Thomas A. Jones*)

18. Place a period after Roman numerals, Arabic numbers, and letters of the alphabet in an outline. (*II., IV., 5., 25., A., B.*)

SECTION 7: APOSTROPHES

19. Form a contraction by using an apostrophe in place of a letter or letters that have been left out. (*I'll, he's, isn't, wasn't, can't*)

20. Form the possessive of singular and plural nouns by using an apostrophe. (*boy's baseball, boys' baseball, children's baseball*)

21. Form the plurals of letters, symbols, numbers, and signs with the apostrophe plus *s* (*'s*). (*9's, B's, b's*)

SECTION 8: UNDERLINING

22. Use underlining or italics for titles of books, magazines, works of art, ships, newspapers, motion pictures, etc. (*A famous movie is <u>Gone With the Wind</u>. Our newspaper is the <u>Cabot Star Herald</u>.*) (*<u>Titanic</u>, <u>Charlotte's Web</u>, etc.*)

SECTION 9: QUOTATION MARKS

23. Use quotation marks to set off the titles of songs, short stories, short poems, articles, essays, short plays, and book chapters. (*Do you like to sing the song "America" in music class?*)

24. Quotation marks are used at the beginning and end of the person's words to separate what the person actually said from the rest of the sentence. Since the quotation tells what is being said, it will always have quotation marks around it.

25. The words that tell who is speaking are the explanatory words. Do not set explanatory words off with quotation marks. (*Fred said, "I'm here."*) (**Fred said** *are explanatory words and should not be set off with quotations.*)

26. A new paragraph is used to indicate a change of speaker.

27. When a speaker's speech is longer than one paragraph, quotation marks are used at the beginning of each paragraph and at the end of the last paragraph of that speaker's speech.

28. Use single quotation marks to enclose a quotation within a quotation. *"My teddy bear says 'I love you' four different ways," said little Amy.*

29. Use a period at the end of explanatory words that come at the end of a sentence.

30. Use a comma to separate a direct quotation from the explanatory words.

Reference 38: Three-Point Paragraph and Three-Paragraph Essay	
Outline of a Three-Point Paragraph	**Outline of a Three-Paragraph Essay**
I. Title	I. Title
II. Paragraph (9 sentences)	II. Paragraph 1 - Introduction (3 sentences)
A. Topic sentence	A. Topic and general number sentence
B. A three-point sentence	B. Extra information about the topic sentence
C. A **first-point** sentence	C. Three-point sentence
D. A **supporting** sentence for the 1st point	III. Paragraph 2 - Body (6-9 sentences)
E. A **second-point** sentence	A. **First-point** sentence
F. A **supporting** sentence for the 2nd point	B. One or two **supporting** sentences for the 1st point
G. A **third-point** sentence	C. **Second-point** sentence
H. A **supporting** sentence for the 3rd point	D. One or two **supporting** sentences for the 2nd point
I. A concluding sentence	E. **Third-point** sentence
	F. One or two **supporting** sentences for the 3rd point
	IV. Paragraph 3 - Conclusion (2 sentences)
	A. Concluding general statement
	B. Concluding summary sentence

Reference 39: Steps in Writing a Three-Paragraph Expository Essay

WRITING TOPIC: State Parks

LIST THE POINTS FOR THE TOPIC

♦ Select three points to list about the topic.
    1. exploration
    2. education
    3. relaxation

WRITING THE INTRODUCTION AND TITLE

1. Sentence #1 – Topic Sentence

Write the topic sentence by using the words in your topic and adding a general number word, such as *several, many, some,* or *numerous,* instead of the exact number of points you will discuss.

(I have discovered that state parks are beneficial in many ways.)

2. Sentence #2 – Extra Information about the topic sentence

This sentence can clarify, explain, define, or just be an extra interesting comment about the topic sentence. If you need another sentence to complete your information, write an extra sentence here. If you write an extra sentence, your introductory paragraph will have four sentences in it instead of three.

(Although many people believe entertainment is found only through technology and its advances, I think nature can be just as entertaining.)

Reference 39: Steps in Writing a Three-Paragraph Expository Essay (continued)

3. Sentence #3 – Three-point sentence

This sentence will list the three points to be discussed in the order that you will present them in the body of your paper. You can list the points with or without the specific number in front.

(State parks provide opportunities for exploration, education, and relaxation for everyone.) or (The three reasons why I enjoy state parks are that they provide opportunities for exploration, education, and relaxation for everyone.)

♦ The Title – Since there are many possibilities for titles, look at the topic and the three points listed about the topic. Use some of the words in the topic and write a phrase to tell what your paragraph is about. Your title can be short or long. Capitalize the first, last, and important words in your title. **(The Benefits of State Parks)**

WRITING THE BODY

4. Sentence #4 – First Point – Write a sentence stating your first point.

(One of the reasons I enjoy state parks is that they allow for endless exploration of nature.)

5. Sentence #5 – Supporting Sentence(s) – Write one or two sentences that give more information about your first point.

(Each park offers various landscapes and a variety of wildlife for one to seek out and explore.)

6. Sentence #6 – Second Point – Write a sentence stating your second point.

(Another reason I enjoy state parks is that they offer a wonderful opportunity for education.)

7. Sentence #7 – Supporting Sentence(s) – Write one or two sentences that give more information about your second point.

(Upon arrival, each park becomes an outdoor classroom filled with sights, sounds, smells, and hands-on experience.)

8. Sentence #8 – Third Point – Write a sentence stating your third point.

(I also enjoy state parks because they are the perfect place for a relaxing vacation.)

9. Sentence #9 – Supporting Sentence(s) – Write one or two sentences that give more information about your third point.

(Whether you spend a weekend on the lake or a week camping in the mountains, there is no better place to relax than at a state park.)

WRITING THE CONCLUSION

10. Sentence #10 – Concluding General Statement – Read the topic sentence again and then rewrite it, using some of the same words to say the same thing in a different way.

(Clearly, state parks have many advantages.)

11. Sentence #11 – Concluding Summary (Final) Sentence – Read the three-point sentence again and then rewrite it using some of the same words to say the same thing in a different way.

(For those who enjoy the beauty of nature, state parks can be very exhilarating.)

Reference 39: Steps in Writing a Three-Paragraph Expository Essay (continued)

SAMPLE THREE-PARAGRAPH ESSAY

The Benefits of State Parks

I have discovered that state parks are beneficial in many ways. Although many people believe entertainment is found only through technology and its advances, I think nature can be just as entertaining. State parks provide opportunities for exploration, education, and relaxation for everyone.

One of the reasons I enjoy state parks is that they allow for endless exploration of nature. Each park offers various landscapes and a variety of wildlife for one to seek out and explore. Another reason I enjoy state parks is that they offer a wonderful opportunity for education. Upon arrival, each park becomes an outdoor classroom filled with sights, sounds, smells, and hands-on experience. I also enjoy state parks because they are the perfect place for a relaxing vacation. Whether you spend a weekend on the lake or a week camping in the mountains, there is no better place to relax than at a state park.

Clearly, state parks have many advantages. For those who enjoy the beauty of nature, state parks can be very exhilarating.

Reference 40: Persuasive Paragraph and Essay Guidelines

Guidelines for a Persuasive Paragraph

Paragraph (10-13 sentences)

A. **Topic** sentence (opinion statement)
B. **General number** sentence
C. **First-point** persuasive sentence
D. 1 or 2 **supporting** sentences for the 1st point
E. **Second-point** persuasive sentence
F. 1 or 2 **supporting** sentences for the 2nd point
G. **Third-point** persuasive sentence
H. 1 or 2 **supporting** sentences for the 3rd point
I. **In conclusion** sentence (Repeat topic idea)
J. **Final summary** sentence
(Summarize reasons)

Guidelines for a 3-Paragraph Persuasive Essay

I. Paragraph 1 – Introduction   (3 sentences)
  A. **Topic** sentence   (opinion statement)
  B. **Reason** sentence
  C. **General number** sentence
II. Paragraph 2 – Body   (6-9 sentences)
  A. **First-point** persuasive sentence
  B. 1 or 2 **supporting** sentences for the 1st point
  C. **Second-point** persuasive sentence
  D. 1 or 2 **supporting** sentences for the 2nd point
  E. **Third-point** persuasive sentence
  F. 1 or 2 **supporting** sentences for the 3rd point
III. Paragraph 3 – Conclusion   (2 sentences)
  A. **In conclusion** sentence   (Repeat topic idea)
  B. **Final summary** sentence (Summarize reasons)

Cooking

Everyone should learn how to cook. Although cooking is an essential part of our survival, it can also be very rewarding. There are numerous reasons why learning to cook is beneficial.

The first benefit of learning to cook is that cooking is an enjoyable and easy form of education. Without realizing it, you can easily learn different forms of measurements, time, temperature, and even fractions. The second benefit of learning to cook is the variety that this hobby offers. Thousands of recipes are available to amateurs and professionals alike. The third benefit of learning to cook is self-satisfaction. Not only do you feel a sense of value in what you have accomplished, but you can also share your bounty with others.

In conclusion, everyone should learn to cook, not only out of necessity, but also for the pleasure and pride in a job well done. Without a doubt, cooking is a great mixture of education and fun.

Reference 41: Direct Object, Verb-transitive, and Pattern 2

1. A **direct object** is a noun or pronoun after the verb that completes the meaning of the sentence.
2. A **direct object** is labeled as **DO**.
3. To find the **direct object**, ask WHAT or WHOM after the verb.
4. A **direct object** must be verified to mean someone or something different from the subject noun.
5. A **verb-transitive** is an action verb with a direct object after it and is labeled V-t.
   (Whatever receives the action of a transitive verb is the direct object.)

Sample Sentence for the exact words to say to find the direct object and transitive verb.

1. The children built a snowman.
2. Who built a snowman? children - SN
3. What is being said about children? children built - V
4. Children built what? snowman - verify the noun
5. Does snowman mean the same thing as children? No.
6. Snowman - DO
   (Say: Snowman - direct object.)
7. Built - V-t
   (Say: Built - verb-transitive.)
8. A - A

9. The - A
10. SN V-t DO P2 Check
    (Say: Subject Noun, Verb-transitive, Direct Object, Pattern 2, Check. This first check is to make sure the "t" is added to the verb.)
11. Verb-transitive - check again.
    ("Check again" means to check for prepositional phrases and then go through the rest of the Question and Answer Flow.)
12. No prepositional phrases.
13. Period, statement, declarative sentence
14. Go back to the verb - divide the complete subject from the complete predicate.

Reference 42: Regular Editing Checklist

Read each sentence and go through the Sentence Checkpoints below.

_____ E1. Sentence sense check. (Check for words left out or words repeated.)

_____ E2. First word, capital letter check. End mark check. Any other capitalization check. Any other punctuation check.

_____ E3. Sentence structure and punctuation check.
(Check for correct construction and correct punctuation of a simple sentence, a simple sentence with compound parts, or a compound sentence.)

_____ E4. Spelling and homonym check.
(Check for misspelled words and incorrect homonym choices.)

_____ E5. Usage check.
(Check subject-verb agreement, a/an choice, double negatives, verb tenses, and contractions.)

Read each paragraph and go through the Paragraph Checkpoints below.

_____ E6. Check to see that each paragraph is indented.

_____ E7. Check each paragraph for a topic sentence.

_____ E8. Check each sentence to make sure it supports the topic of the paragraph.

_____ E9. Check the content for interest and creativity.

_____ E10. Check the type and format of the writing assigned.

Reference 43: Editing Example

Topic: **Reasons why amusement parks are so much fun**
Three main points: **(1. Thrilling rides   2. Entertaining games   3. Tasty snacks)**

Amusement   P
The Amusing Amusemant park

→   a   (.) T   reasons   so
People everywhere love to visit Amusement parks for various reasons three reason amusement parks are sew much
        (,)   (,)   offer(.)
fun are the thrilling rides the entertaining games and the tasty snacks that amusement parks offers
                              is   coasters
    The first reason amusement parks are so much fun are the thrilling rides. From roller costers to tilt-a-whirls, each
       variety   anyone's   no comma
park offers a wide vareity of rides to match anyones style. The second reason amusement parks are so much fun,
is   knock
Is the number of entertaining games. A couple of dollars gives you the chance to nock down a target with a baseball
      animal   is
and win a huge stuffed anamal. The third reason amusement parks are so much fun are the tasty snacks. The
    an   lemonade   (,)
park contains a abundance of concession stands that offer fresh squeezed lemonaide, hot funnel cakes fluffy
cotton   (.)
cotten candy, and sticky caramel apples
         are   reasons   (,)
    In conclusion, amusement parks is entertaining for many reason. The thrilling rides, entertaining games and tasty
no comma   an
snacks, make the amusement parks a exceptionally fun place to visit.

Total Mistakes: 31
Editing Guide: Sentence checkpoints: **E1, E2, E3, E4, E5**   Paragraph checkpoints: **E6, E7, E8, E9, E10**

Reference 44: Complete Sentences and Sentence Fragments

PART 1: Identifying Sentences and Fragments

Identifying simple sentences and fragments: Write **S** for a complete sentence and **F** for a sentence fragment on the line beside each group of words below.

S	1.	The zebra ran swiftly.
F	2.	During the show.
S	3.	The cruiser sailed.
F	4.	Asking for our support.
F	5.	The green house on the corner.

PART 2: Sentence Fragments

Fragment Examples: (1) growled at the cat (2) the two bear cubs (3) after I fell (4) watching the baby.

PART 3: Correcting Sentence Fragments

Directions: Add the part that is underlined in parentheses to make each fragment into a complete sentence.

1. On a lily pad in the pond. (subject part, predicate part, <u>both the subject and the predicate</u>)
(**The frog dozed** on a lily pad in the pond.)

2. The nasty storm. (subject part, <u>predicate part</u>, both the subject and the predicate)
(The nasty storm **toppled trees in the night**.)

3. Glued a gold star on my paper. (<u>subject part</u>, predicate part, both the subject and the predicate)
(**The teacher** glued a gold star on my paper.)

Reference 45: Simple Sentences, Compound Parts, and Fragments

Example 1: The red ball bounced slowly down the hill. (**S**)
Example 2: <u>Julie and Amanda</u> work at the restaurant. (**SCS**)
Example 3: Alex <u>painted and decorated</u> the birdhouse. (**SCV**)

Part 2: Identify each kind of sentence by writing the abbreviation in the blank. (**S, SS, F, SCS, SCV**)

SCV 1. The children laughed and cheered for the magician.
SCS 2. The pen and pencil were left on the desk.
F 3. Before we move to Atlanta.
S 4. The birds made their nests in the trees.
SS 5. I turned on the oven. It heated up the cold room.

Part 3: Put a slash to separate each run-on sentence below. Then, correct the run-on sentences by rewriting them as indicated by the labels in parentheses at the end of each sentence.

1. The young woman was walking **/** her car ran out of gas. (**SS**)
The young woman was walking. Her car ran out of gas.

2. The picture is on the mantel **/** the clock is on the mantel. (**SCS**)
The picture and the clock are on the mantel.

3. The toddler rolled in the snow **/** she played in the snow for hours. (**SCV**)
The toddler rolled and played in the snow for hours.

Reference 46: The Compound Sentence

1. Compound means two. A compound sentence is two complete sentences joined together correctly with a comma and a conjunction. The abbreviation for a compound sentence is **CD**.

2. <u>One way to join two sentences</u> and make a compound sentence is to <u>use a comma and a conjunction</u>. The formula for you to follow will always be given at the end of the sentence. The formula gives the abbreviation for the compound sentence and lists the conjunction to use (**CD, and**). (The three most commonly-used conjunctions are **and, but, or**.) Remember to place the comma BEFORE the conjunction.

Example: We picked vegetables from the **garden, and** we ate them for dinner. (CD, and)

3. Compound sentences should be closely related in thought and importance.

Correct: We picked vegetables from the **garden, and** we ate them for dinner.
Incorrect: We picked vegetables from the **garden, and** my baby brother doesn't like cheese.

Reference 47: Using SCS, SCV, and CD Correctly

Put a slash to separate the two complete thoughts in each run-on sentence. Correct the run-on sentences or fragments as indicated by the labels in parentheses at the end of each sentence.

1. Samantha loves amusement parks **/** she doesn't like the roller coasters. (**CD**, but)
   Samantha loves amusement parks, but she doesn't like the roller coasters.

2. My uncle owns a pizza parlor **/** the food is delicious! (**CD**, and)
   My uncle owns a pizza parlor, and the food is delicious!

3. Beth works in the church kitchen **/** Mary works in the church kitchen. (**SCS**)
   Beth and Mary work in the church kitchen. *(When the subject is compound, the verb is plural.)*

4. For extra money, Susan walks dogs **/** she watches children. (**SCV**)
   For extra money, Susan walks dogs and watches children.

Reference 48: Identifying S, F, SCS, SCV, and CD

Part 1: Identify each kind of sentence by writing the abbreviation in the blank (**S, F, SCS, SCV, CD**).

SCV	1. The hungry pup gnawed on his bone and growled.
F	2. Only because no one bid on the property.
CD	3. He was elected senator, but he narrowly won the election.
S	4. Between acts, there was a brief intermission.
SCS	5. Lee and his wife are expecting twins.
CD	6. The fire truck arrived, and an ambulance came shortly thereafter.

Part 2: Use the ways listed below to correct this run-on sentence: **He made a mistake he did not correct it.**

7. CD, but **He made a mistake, but he did not correct it.**   8. SCV **He made a mistake but did not correct it.**

Reference 49: Contraction Chart				Pronoun	Contraction
AM		**HAS**			
I am — I'm		has not — hasn't		**its**	**it's**
		he has — he's		(owns)	(it is)
IS		she has — she's		*its coat*	*it's cute*
is not — isn't					
he is — he's		**HAVE**			
she is — she's		have not — haven't		**your**	**you're**
it is — it's		I have — I've		(owns)	(you are)
who is — who's		you have — you've		*your car*	*you're right*
that is — that's		we have — we've			
what is — what's		they have — they've			
there is — there's				**their**	**they're**
		HAD		(owns)	(they are)
ARE		had not — hadn't		*their house*	*they're gone*
are not — aren't		I had — I'd			
you are — you're		he had — he'd			
we are — we're		she had — she'd		**whose**	**who's**
they are — they're		you had — you'd		(owns)	(who is)
		we had — we'd		*whose cat*	*who's going*
WAS, WERE		they had — they'd			
was not — wasn't					
were not — weren't		**WILL, SHALL**			
		will not — won't			
DO, DOES, DID		I will — I'll			
do not — don't		he will — he'll			
does not — doesn't		she will — she'll			
did not — didn't		you will — you'll			
		we will — we'll			
CAN		they will — they'll			
cannot — can't					
		WOULD			
LET		would not — wouldn't			
let us — let's		I would — I'd			
		he would — he'd			
		she would — she'd			
		you would — you'd			
		we would — we'd			
		they would — they'd			
		SHOULD, COULD			
		should not — shouldn't			
		could not — couldn't			

Reference 50: Linking Verbs

An action verb shows action. It tells what the subject does. A linking verb does not show action. It does not tell what the subject does. A linking verb is called a state of being verb because it tells **what the subject is or is like**. A **linking verb** is identified with the abbreviation **LV**. To decide if a verb is linking or action, remember these two things:

1. A linking verb connects the subject to a noun in the predicate that means the same thing as the subject.

A predicate noun is a noun in the predicate that means the same thing as the subject. The subject and predicate noun are connected by a linking verb. A **predicate noun** is identified with the abbreviation **PrN**.

(Mrs. Land is the teacher.)   *(They are the actors.)*   *(Sue is the friend.)*   *(Uncle is the mayor.)*

| SN | LV | PrN | SP LV | PrN | SN LV | PrN | SN LV | PrN |

Mrs. Land **is** my (teacher).   They **are** famous (actors).   Sue **is** my new (friend).   My uncle **is** the town (mayor).

2. A linking verb connects the subject to an adjective in the predicate that describes the subject.

A predicate adjective is an adjective in the predicate that describes the subject. The subject and predicate adjective are connected by a linking verb. A **predicate adjective** is identified with the abbreviation **PA**.

(What kind of tree? tall)   *(What kind of Kay? thirsty)*   *(What kind of apple? red)*   *(What kind of they? envious)*

| SN LV PA | SN LV PA | SN LV PA | SP LV | PA |

The tree **is** (tall).   Kay **was** (thirsty).   The apple **is** (red).   They **were** very (envious).

These are the <u>most common</u> linking verbs: *am, is, are, was, were, be, been, seem, become.*
These <u>sensory verbs</u> can be linking or action: *taste, sound, smell, feel, look.*

A good rule to follow:
If a sentence has a predicate noun (PrN) or a predicate adjective (PA), it has a linking verb.
If a sentence <u>does not have</u> a predicate noun (PrN) or a predicate adjective (PA), it probably has an action verb.

Example: Underline each subject and fill in each column according to the title. Write **L** for linking verb or **A** for action verb

	List each Verb	Write PrN, PA, or None	Write L or A
1. The <u>roads</u> are wet.	are	PA	L
2. The <u>train</u> moves quickly down the rails.	moves	None	A
3. <u>Terra</u> is my new roommate.	is	PrN	L
4. The <u>gnat</u> is buzzing my ear.	is buzzing	None	A

Reference 51: Similes and Metaphors

When a writer uses words to draw a picture of two things that he is comparing, it is called a figure of speech. Two figures of speech that writers use most often are **simile** and **metaphor**.

<u>A simile</u> draws a picture by comparing one noun to another noun in the sentence using "like" or "as."

Examples: Regina's glare was as cold as ice. Her smile was as bright as the sun.
His hands shook like leaves. The boys swing from the branches like monkeys.

<u>A metaphor</u> draws a picture by showing how two very different things can be alike. It will use linking verbs (*am, is, are, was, were*) to connect the noun in the predicate to the subject.

Examples: Her homemade chili was fire that burned in my stomach.
The snow is a blanket on our lawn.

Reference 52: Quotation Rules for Beginning Quotes

1. **Pattern:** "C -quote- (,!?) " <u>explanatory words</u> (.)
   (Quotation marks, capital letter, quote, end punctuation choice, quotation marks closed, explanatory words, period)

2. Underline **end explanatory words** and use a period at the end.

3. You should see the **beginning quote** – Use quotation marks at the beginning and end of what is said. Then, put a comma, question mark, or exclamation point (no period) after the quote but in front of the quotation marks.

4. **Capitalize** the first word of the quote, any proper nouns, or the pronoun I.

5. **Punctuate** the rest of the sentence by checking for any apostrophes, periods, or commas that may be needed within the sentence.

Guided Practice

Sentence: **the space shuttle will land a day late capt walker stated**

1. Pattern: "C -quote- (,!?) " <u>explanatory words</u> (.)

2. the space shuttle will land a day late **<u>capt walker stated</u>**(.)

3. "the space shuttle will land a day late**,**" <u>capt walker stated</u>.

4. "**T**he space shuttle will land a day late," <u>**C**apt **W**alker stated</u>.

5. "The space shuttle will land a day late," <u>**Capt.** Walker stated</u>.

6. **Corrected Sentence:** "The space shuttle will land a day late," Capt. Walker stated.

Reference 53: Quotation Rules for End Quotes

1. **Pattern:** <u>C</u> - explanatory words(,) "**C** -quote- (.!?) "
   (Capital letter, explanatory words, comma, quotation marks, capital letter, quote, end punctuation choice, quotation marks closed)

2. Underline **beginning explanatory words** and use a comma after them.

3. You should see the **end quote** – Use quotation marks at the beginning and end of what is said. Then, put a period, question mark, or exclamation point (no comma) after the quote, but in front of the quotation marks.

4. **Capitalize** the first of the explanatory words at the beginning of a sentence, the first word of the quote, and any proper nouns or the pronoun *I*.

5. **Punctuate** the rest of the sentence by checking for any apostrophes, periods, or commas that may be needed within the sentence.

Guided Practice

Sentence: capt walker stated the space shuttle will land a day late

1. Pattern: <u>C</u> -explanatory words(,) "**C** -quote- (.!?) "

2. <u>**capt walker stated**(,)</u> the space shuttle will land a day late

3. <u>capt walker stated</u>, "the space shuttle will land a day late**. "**

4. <u>**Ca**pt **W**alker stated</u>, "**T**he space shuttle will land a day late."

5. <u>**Capt.** Walker stated</u>, "The space shuttle will land a day late."

6. **Corrected Sentence:** Capt. Walker stated, "The space shuttle will land a day late."

Reference 54: Story Elements Outline

1. **Main Idea (Tell the problem or situation that needs a solution.)**
   Allen is waiting on his little brother so they can play baseball.

2. **Setting (Tell when and where the story takes place, either clearly stated or implied.)**
   When – The story takes place in the afternoon. Where – The story takes place at the Marshall's house.

3. **Characters (Tell whom or what the story is about.)**
   The main characters are Allen and Calvin Marshall.

4. **Plot (Tell what the characters in the story do and what happens to them.)**
   The story is about a boy's frustrating experience with a younger sibling.

5. **Ending (Use a strong ending that will bring the story to a close.)**
   The story ends with Allen leaving ahead of his brother to go to the ball field.

Big Brother

Following an afternoon snack, the Marshall brothers, Allen and Calvin, prepared to leave the house to play baseball in the schoolyard. Allen quickly gathered his baseball gear and waited patiently for his brother on the front porch. He tossed his bat onto his shoulders and began to whistle a tune.

Meanwhile, Calvin rushed around the house looking for his shoes and his lucky baseball cap. He grabbed a couple of worn-out baseballs; then, he darted onto the front porch without his shoes. He quickly dropped the baseballs and his cap on the front steps and rushed back into the house for his shoes.

Allen just rolled his eyes and sighed. He had already waited on his little brother for ten minutes. He impatiently looked at his watch and began the long journey to the schoolyard. He knew his brother would eventually catch up with him.

Reference 55: Regular and Irregular Verbs

Most verbs are **regular verbs**. This means that they form the past tense merely by adding **-ed**, **-d**, or **-t** to the main verb: *race, raced*. This simple procedure makes regular verbs easy to identify. Some verbs, however, do not form their past tense this way. For that reason, they are called **irregular verbs**. Most irregular verbs form the past tense by having a **vowel spelling change** in the word. For example: *br<u>ea</u>k, br<u>o</u>ke, br<u>o</u>ken* or *s<u>i</u>ng, s<u>a</u>ng, s<u>u</u>ng*.

To decide if a verb is regular or irregular, remember these two things:

1. Look only at the main verb. If the main verb is made past tense with an *-ed, -d, or -t* ending, it is a regular verb. (*trace, traced, traced*)
2. Look only at the main verb. If the main verb is made past tense with a vowel spelling change, it is an irregular verb. (*sink, sank, sunk*)

A partial listing of the most common irregular verbs is on the irregular verb chart located in Reference 31 on page 25 in the student book. Refer to this chart whenever necessary.

Identify each verb as regular or irregular and put **R** or **I** in the blank. Then, write the past tense form.

| fly | _I_ | _flew_ | move | _R_ | _moved_ | tell | _I_ | _told_ |
| build | _R_ | _built_ | freeze | _I_ | _froze_ | enjoy | _R_ | _enjoyed_ |

Reference 56: Simple Verb Tenses

When you are writing paragraphs, you must use verbs that are in the same tense. Tense means time. The tense of a verb shows the time of the action. There are three basic tenses that show when an action takes place. They are **present tense, past tense,** and **future tense**. These tenses are known as the simple tenses.

1. The **simple present tense** shows that something is happening now, in the present. The present tense form usually ends in *s, es,* or in a *plain ending*.

   (Regular present tense form: cover, covers) (Irregular present tense form: swim, swims)
   (**Examples:** Piles of snow <u>cover</u> the sidewalk. Jeff <u>swims</u> in the lake everyday.)

2. The **simple past tense** shows that something has happened sometime in the past. The regular past tense form usually ends in *-ed, -d,* or *-t*. Most irregular past tense forms should be memorized.

   (Regular past tense form: covered) (Irregular past tense form: swam)
   (**Examples:** Piles of snow <u>covered</u> the sidewalk. Jeff <u>swam</u> in the lake everyday.)

3. The **future tense** shows that something will happen sometime in the future. The future tense form always has the helping verb *will* or *shall* before the main verb.

   (Regular future tense form: will cover) (Irregular future tense form: will swim)
   (**Examples:** Piles of snow <u>will cover</u> the sidewalk. Jeff <u>will swim</u> in the lake everyday.)

Simple Present Tense	Simple Past Tense	Simple Future Tense
What to look for: **one verb** with s, es, or plain ending.	What to look for: **one verb** with -ed, -d, -t or irr spelling change.	What to look for: **will** or **shall** with a main verb.
1. He <u>moves</u> to the inside.	1. He <u>moved</u> to the inside.	1. He <u>will move</u> to the inside.
2. He <u>does</u> electrical work.	2. He <u>did</u> electrical work.	2. He <u>will do</u> electrical work.

Reference 57: Tenses of Helping Verbs

1. If there is only a main verb in a sentence, the tense is determined by the main verb and will be either present tense or past tense.
2. If there is a helping verb with a main verb, the tense of both verbs will be determined by the helping verb, not the main verb.

Since the helping verb determines a verb's tense, it is important to learn the tenses of the 14 helping verbs you will be using. You should memorize the list below so you will never have trouble with tenses.

Present tense helping verbs: am, is, are, has, have, does, do
Past tense helping verbs: was, were, had, did, been
Future tense helping verbs: will, shall

If you use a present tense helping verb, it is considered present tense even though the main verb has an -*ed* ending, and it doesn't sound like present tense. (*I have walked - present tense.*) In later grades, you will learn that certain helping verbs help form other tenses called the perfect tenses.

Example 1: Underline each verb or verb phrase. Identify the verb tense by writing a number **1** for present tense, a number **2** for past tense, or a number **3** for future tense. Write the past tense form and **R** or **I** for Regular or Irregular.

Verb Tense		Main Verb Past Tense Form	R or I
1	1. My parents <u>have gone</u> to the store.	went	I
2	2. She <u>had walked</u> several miles.	walked	R
3	3. The theater <u>will open</u> next week.	opened	R

Example 2: List the present tense and past tense helping verbs below.

Present tense:	1. **am**	2. **is**	3. **are**	4. **has**	5. **have**	6. **does**	7. **do**
Past tense:	8. **was**	9. **were**	10. **had**	11. **did**	12. **been**		

Reference 58: Changing Tenses in Paragraphs

Guided Example 1: Change the underlined present tense verbs in Paragraph 1 to past tense verbs in Paragraph 2.

Paragraph 1: Present Tense

Annie **rides** her bike every afternoon. She **is** very careful, and she **watches** eagerly for her grandmother. At the end of the block, her grandmother **is waiting** for her and **waves** happily. Together, they **sit** on the porch and **munch** several of Grandma's homemade cookies.

Paragraph 2: Past Tense

Annie **rode** her bike every afternoon. She **was** very careful, and she **watched** eagerly for her grandmother. At the end of the block, her grandmother **was waiting** for her and **waved** happily. Together, they **sat** on the porch and **munched** several of Grandma's homemade cookies.

Guided Example 2: Change the underlined mixed tense verbs in Paragraph 3 to present tense verbs in Paragraph 4.

Paragraph 3: Mixed Tenses

Dimples **was** the name of my cat. She **loved** to sleep behind the pillows on our couch. Whenever I **opened** the door, she **dashes** outside and **chased** leaves. Dimples **loves** adventure!

Paragraph 4: Present Tense

Dimples **is** the name of my cat. She **loves** to sleep behind the pillows on our couch. Whenever I **open** the door, she **dashes** outside and **chases** leaves. Dimples **loves** adventure!

Reference 59: Double Negatives

Negative Words That Begin With *N*					Other Negative Words	Negative Prefixes
neither	no	no one	not (n't)	nowhere	barely, hardly, scarcely	dis, non, un
never	nobody	none	nothing			

Three Ways to Correct a Double Negative

Rule 1: Change the second negative to a positive:
Wrong: We **couldn't** find **no** money.   Right: We **couldn't** find **any** money.

Rule 2: Take out the negative part of a contraction:
Wrong: We **couldn't** find **no** money.   Right: We **could** find **no** money.

Rule 3: Remove the first negative word (possibility of a verb change):
Wrong: We **couldn't** find **no** money.   Right: We **found no** money.

Changing Negative Words to Positive Words

1. Change *no* or *none* to *any*.
2. Change *nobody* to *anybody*.
3. Change *no one* to *anyone*.
4. Change *nothing* to *anything*.
5. Change *nowhere* to *anywhere*.
6. Change *never* to *ever*.
7. Change *neither* to *either*.
8. Remove the *n't* from a contraction.

Examples: Underline the negative words in each sentence. Rewrite each sentence and correct the double-negative mistake as indicated by the rule number in parentheses at the end of the sentence.

1. He <u>didn't</u> have <u>no</u> homework. (Rule 3) **He had no homework.**

2. The children <u>couldn't</u> <u>hardly</u> wait for the party. (Rule 2) **The children could hardly wait for the party.**

3. She <u>didn't</u> order <u>nothing</u> for dessert. (Rule 1) **She didn't order anything for dessert.**

Reference 60: Rules for the Plurals of Nouns with Different Endings

1. "ch, sh, z, s, ss, x" – add "es."
2. a vowel plus "y," add an "s."
3. a consonant plus "y," change "y" to "i" and add "es."
4. "f" or "fe," change the "f" or "fe" to "v" and add "es."
5. irregular nouns – change spellings completely.
6. "f" or "ff," add "s."
7. a vowel plus "o," add "s."
8. a consonant plus "o," add "es."
9. stays the same for S and P.
10. regular nouns – add "s."

Use the rules above to write the correct plural form of these nouns:

	Rule	Plural Form			Rule	Plural Form
1. key	2	**keys**	3. roof		6	**roofs**
2. shelf	4	**shelves**	4. fish		1 or 9	**fish or fishes**

Reference 61: Guidelines for Descriptive Writing

1. **When describing people,** it is helpful to notice these types of details: appearance, walk, voice, manner, gestures, personality traits, any special incident related to the person being described, and any striking details that make that person stand out in your mind.

2. **When describing places or things,** it is helpful to notice these types of details: the physical features of a place or thing (color, texture, smell, shape, size, age), any unusual features, any special incident related to the place or thing being described, and whether or not the place or thing is special to you.

3. **When describing nature,** it is helpful to notice these types of details: the special features of the season, the sights, smells, sounds, colors, animals, insects, birds, and any special incident related to the scene being described.

4. **When describing an incident or an event,** it is helpful to notice these types of details: the order in which the event takes place, any specific facts that will keep the story moving from a beginning to an ending, the answers to any of the *who, what, when, where, why,* and *how* questions that the reader needs to know, and especially the details that will create a clear picture, such as how things look, sound, smell, feel, etc.

Reference 62: Descriptive Paragraph Guidelines

A. Sentence 1 is the topic sentence that introduces **what is being described**.

B. For sentences 2-8, use **the descriptive details** in Reference 61.

C. Sentence 9 is a concluding sentence that **restates, or relates back to, the topic sentence.**

A Trip to the Supermarket

Almost every week, Mom makes a trip to the supermarket, and my little brother and I go with her. Before we leave, Mom hurries around the kitchen making a list of all the groceries that we need. I put on my socks and shoes, and then I help Joey with his. We all pile into our mini van and travel into town. When we arrive at the supermarket, Mom puts Joey in the basket, and I walk beside her. By the time we have finished shopping, my legs are tired. The check-out line is my favorite part of the whole trip, even though the lines are always long. Mom lets Joey and me pick out our favorite treat to eat on our way home. After the grocer sacks all our food, we happily head out to our mini van with a smile on our face and a sweet treat in our hand.

Reference 63: The Five Parts of a Friendly Letter

1. Heading
1. Box or street address of writer
2. City, state, zip code of writer
3. Date letter was written
4. Placement: upper right-hand corner

2. Friendly Greeting or Salutation
1. Begins with *Dear*
2. Names person receiving the letter
3. Has comma after person's name
4. Placement: at left margin, two lines below heading

3. Body
1. Tells reason the letter was written
2. Can have one or more paragraphs
3. Has indented paragraphs
4. Is placed one line below the greeting
5. Skips one line between each paragraph

4. Closing
1. Closes letter with a personal phrase (Your friend, With love,)
2. Capitalizes only first word
3. Is followed by a comma
4. Is placed two lines below the body
5. Begins just to the right of the middle of the letter

5. Signature
1. Tells who wrote the letter
2. Is usually signed in cursive
3. Uses first name only unless there is a question as to which friend or relative you are
4. Is placed beneath the closing

Friendly Letter Example

1. **Heading**
67 Edgewood Court
Madison, KY 38287
August 21, 20____

2. **Friendly Greeting, (or Salutation)**
Dear Tim,

3. **Body (Indent Paragraphs)**

Jon's team, as you may know, made it to the championship finals last weekend. The team will play in Tucson, Arizona, next weekend for the winner's trophy. We are planning to drive to the game and wondered if you'd like to go with us. If so, give me a quick call, and we'll plan to pick you up.

4. **Closing,**
Love,

5. **Signature**
Aunt Tracey

Reference 64: Friendly Envelope Parts

Envelope Parts	Friendly Envelope Example

The return address:
1. Name of the person writing the letter
2. Box or street address of the writer
3. City, state, zip code of the writer

The mailing address:
1. Name of the person receiving the letter
2. Street address of the person receiving the letter
3. City, state, zip of the person receiving the letter

Stamp

| Return Address |
Tracey Lang
67 Edgewood Court
Madison, KY 38287

| Mailing Address |
Tim Tipton
4007 Delaney Drive
Hartsville, TN 75938

Reference 65: Four Types of Business Letters

Four common reasons to write business letters and information about the four types:

1. If you need to send for information - letter of inquiry.

2. If you want to order a product - letter of request or order.

3. If you want to express an opinion - letter to an editor or official.

4. If you want to complain about a product - letter of complaint.

Letter of Inquiry	Letter of Request or Order
1. Ask for information or answers to your questions.	1. Carefully and clearly describe the product.
2. Keep the letter short and to the point.	2. Keep the letter short and to the point.
3. Word the letter so that there can be no question as to what it is you need to know.	3. Include information on how and where the product should be shipped.
	4. Include information on how you will pay for the product.

Letter to an Editor or Official	Letter of Complaint About a Product
1. Clearly explain the problem or situation.	1. Carefully and clearly describe the product.
2. Offer your opinion of the cause and possible solutions.	2. Describe the problem and what may have caused it. (Don't spend too much time explaining how unhappy you are.)
3. Support your opinions with facts and examples.	3. Explain any action you have already taken to solve the problem.
4. Suggest ways to change or improve the situation.	4. End your letter with the action you would like the company to take to solve the problem.

Reference 66: The Six Parts of a Business Letter

1. **Heading:** The heading for a business letter includes the writer's complete address and the full date. The heading is placed in the upper right-hand corner about an inch from the top of the page.

2. **Inside Address:** The inside address includes the name and complete address of the person and/or company you are writing. Place a person's title after his/her name. Separate the title from the name with a comma. If the title is two or more words, place the title separately on the next line. The inside address is placed two lines below the heading on the left side of the page.

3. **Formal Greeting or Salutation:** A formal greeting is placed two lines below the inside address. For a specific person, use a greeting like Dear Mr. (*last name*) or Ms. (*last name*). For a letter addressed to a person by title, use Dear Sir, Dear Madam, or Dear (*Title*). For a company or organization, use Gentlemen, Dear Sirs, or Dear (*Company name*). Place a colon at the end of a business greeting. (*Check the first line of the inside address to determine the right greeting to use.*)

4. **Body:** The information in the body of any business letter should be clearly and briefly written. Skip a line between each paragraph. The body of the business letter is placed two lines below the greeting.

5. **Closing:** Use a formal phrase for a business letter closing (*Very truly, Yours truly, Sincerely, etc.*). Place a comma at the end of the closing. The closing is placed two lines below the body of the letter, on the right.

6. **Signature:** A business letter ends by signing your name beneath the closing. If you are typing your letter, skip four lines and type your full name. Then, write your signature between the closing and your typed name.

Reference 67: Business Letter Example

1. HEADING

26 Bailey Road
Columbus, Ohio 43085
August 10, 20___

2. INSIDE ADDRESS

Mr. James Cook, Sales Manager
Barret Furniture
1062 Finley Street
Boise, Idaho 83700

3. FORMAL GREETING, (OR SALUTATION)

Dear Mr. Cook:

4. BODY (INDENT PARAGRAPHS)

Please send us a catalog of your office furniture and accessories. We are planning to purchase new furniture and file cabinets.

5. FORMAL CLOSING,

Sincerely,

6. SIGNATURE

Donald Sinclair

Reference 68: Business Envelope Parts

Envelope Parts	Business Envelope Example
The return address: 1. Name of the person writing the letter 2. Box or street address of the writer 3. City, state, zip code of the writer	**Return Address** Donald Sinclair 26 Bailey Road Columbus, Ohio 43085
The mailing address: 1. Name of the person receiving the letter 2. Name of the company receiving the letter 3. Street address of the person receiving the letter 4. City, state, zip of the person receiving the letter	**Mailing Address** Mr. James Cook, Sales Manager Barret Furniture 1062 Finley Street Boise, Idaho 83700

Reference 69: Thank-You Notes	
For a Gift	**For an Action**
What - Thank you for... (tell color, kind, and item)	**What -** Thank you for... (tell action)
Use - Tell how the gift is used.	**Helped -** Tell how the action helped.
Thanks - I appreciate your remembering me with this special gift.	**Thanks -** I appreciate your thinking of me at this time.

Example 1: Gift

62 Palmetto Drive
Orlando, Florida 12478
April 23, 20__

Dear Brad,

Do I ever like those awesome binoculars you sent me for my birthday! I've already watched two launches at the Kennedy Space Center. Through the binoculars, it was an amazing sight. Thanks so much.

Your cousin,

Tyler

Example 2: Action

6156 Turquoise Lane
Phoenix, Arizona 46145
June 4, 20__

Dear Jeffrey,

Thanks so much for volunteering to flag traffic while the city workers installed a new flagpole in the village green. The concrete mixers could never have gotten in and out without your help. I look forward to returning the kindness.

Most sincerely,

Marty

Reference 70: Parts of a Book

AT THE FRONT:

1. **Title Page.** This page has the full title of the book, the author's name, the illustrator's name, the name of the publishing company, and the city where the book was published.

2. **Copyright Page.** This page is right after the title page and tells the year in which the book was published and who owns the copyright. If the book has an ISBN number (International Standard Book Number), it is listed here.

3. **Preface** (also called **introduction**). If a book has this page, it will come before the table of contents and will usually tell briefly why the book was written and what it is about.

4. **Table of Contents.** This section lists the major divisions of the book by units or chapters and tells their page numbers.

5. **Body.** This is the main section, or text, of the book.

AT THE BACK:

6. **Appendix.** This section includes extra informative material such as maps, charts, tables, diagrams, letters, etc. It is always wise to find out what is in the appendix, since it may contain supplementary material that you could otherwise find only by going to the library.

7. **Glossary.** This section is like a dictionary and gives the meanings of some of the important words in the book.

8. **Bibliography.** This section includes a list of books used by the author. It could serve as a guide for further reading on a topic.

9. **Index.** This will probably be your most useful section. The purpose of the index is to help you quickly locate information about the topics in the book. It has an alphabetical list of specific topics and tells on which page that information can be found. It is similar to the table of contents, but it is much more detailed.

Reference 71: Main Parts of the Library

Fiction Section

Fiction books contain stories about people, places, or things that are not true. Fiction books are arranged on the shelves in alphabetical order according to the authors' last names. Since fiction stories are made-up, they cannot be used when you research your report topic.

Non-Fiction Section

Non-Fiction books contain information and stories that are true.

Reference Section

The Reference Section is designed to help you find information on many topics. The Reference Section contains many different kinds of reference books and materials. Some of the ones that you need to know about are listed below.

- **Dictionary** (Reference Book)

   The dictionary gives the definition, spelling, pronunciation, and correct usage of words and tells briefly about famous people and places.

- **Encyclopedia** (Reference Book)

   The encyclopedia gives concise, accurate information about persons, places, and events of world-wide interest.

- **Atlas** (Reference Book)

   The atlas is primarily a book of maps, but it often contains facts about oceans, lakes, mountains, areas, population, products, and climates of every part of the world.

- **Almanac** (Reference Book)

   Both *The World Almanac* and the *Information Please Almanac* are published once a year and contain brief, up-to-date information on a variety of topics.

- ***The Readers' Guide to Periodical Literature*** (Reference Book)

   The Readers' Guide to Periodical Literature is an index for magazines. It is a monthly booklet that lists the titles of articles, stories, and poems published in all leading magazines. These titles are listed under topics that are arranged alphabetically. The monthly issues of *The Readers' Guide to Periodical Literature* are bound together in a single volume once a year and filed in the library. By using the *Readers' Guide*, a person researching a topic can know which back issues of magazines might be helpful.

- **Card Catalog** (Reference File)

   The card catalog is a file of cards, arranged alphabetically, and usually placed in the drawers of a cabinet called the card catalog. It is an index to the library. Some libraries now have computer terminals that show the same information as the card catalog, but the information is stored in a computer. Often, the computer listing will also tell whether or not the book is currently on loan from the library.

Reference 72: Alphabetical Order

Example: Put each group of words in alphabetical order. Use numbers to show the order in each column.

Music Words	"B" Words	Math Words	Science Words	"T" Words
2 1. saxophone	**1** 3. Bible	**2** 5. fractions	**2** 7. cell	**1** 9. task
1 2. flute	**2** 4. bike	**1** 6. division	**1** 8. atom	**2** 10. time

---

Reference 73: Guide Words

Example: Below are the tops of two dictionary pages. Write the page number on which each word listed would appear.

canyon (first word)	Page 164	**capitalist** (last word)		**capitalistic** (first word)	Page 165	**captain** (last word)

Page

164 1. capital

165 2. capsule

Reference 74: The Dictionary

1. The words listed in a dictionary are called <u>entry words</u> and are in bold-face type.

2. The <u>entry words</u> are listed in alphabetical order (ABC order).

3. The dictionary tells how to spell the word and how to pronounce the word.

4. The dictionary tells what the word means and gives an example to explain the meaning.

5. The dictionary tells how to use the word and gives the part of speech for the word.

Entry Words

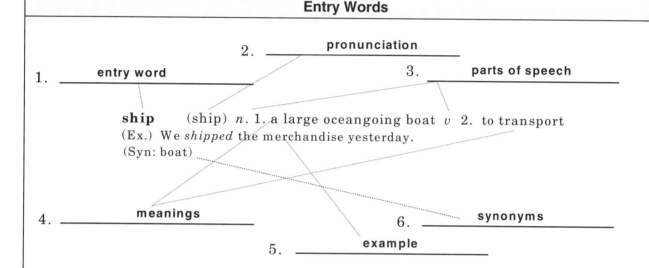

Parts of a Dictionary Entry

1. <u>The entry word</u> – gives correct spelling and divides the word into syllables.

2. <u>Pronunciation</u> – tells how to pronounce a word. It is usually put in parentheses.

3. <u>Part of speech</u> – uses small *n.* for noun, small *v.* for verb, *adj.* for adjective, etc.

4. <u>Meanings</u> – are numbered definitions listed according to the part of speech.

5. <u>Example</u> – a sentence using the entry word to illustrate a meaning. Shown as (Ex.)

6. <u>Synonyms</u> – words that have similar meanings to the entry word. Shown as (Syn:)

Notes

PRACTICE

SECTION

Chapter 1, Lesson 4, Practice: Write *a* or *an* in the blanks.

1. He fried ____ egg for lunch.
2. We saw ____ ambulance.
3. She bought ____ hamburger.
4. The dog needed ____ bath.
5. Allison rode ____ elevator.
6. I chased ____ frog.
7. ____ angel
8. ____ picture
9. ____ owl
10. ____ judge
11. ____ edge
12. ____ flower

Chapter 2, Lesson 4, Practice 1: Match the definitions. Write the correct letter beside each numbered concept.

1. sentences should begin with
2. article adjectives
3. adjective modifies
4. verb question
5. tells what the subject does
6. subject-noun question (thing)
7. article adjectives can be called
8. parts of a complete sentence
9. noun
10. subject-noun question (person)
11. adverb modifies

A. verb, adjective, or adverb
B. who
C. what is being said about
D. person, place, or thing
E. what
F. capital letter
G. subject, verb, complete sense
H. a, an, the
I. noun or pronoun
J. verb
K. noun markers

Chapter 2, Lesson 4, Practice 2: Write *a* or *an* in the blanks.

1. We searched for ____ key.
2. James is ____ author.
3. Pam ate ____ ear of corn.
4. She served ____ bowl of soup.
5. Noah built ____ ark.
6. That is ____ great idea!
7. ____ letter
8. ____ wrinkle
9. ____ ostrich
10. ____ store
11. ____ index
12. ____ apricot

Chapter 3, Lesson 1, Practice 1: Put the end mark and the abbreviation for each kind of sentence in the blanks below.

1. Put the vocabulary words in alphabetical order _____
2. Are you working late tonight _____
3. They found the lost child _____
4. We are moving to Florida _____
5. Mow the lawn for Ms. Brown _____

Chapter 3, Lesson 1, Practice 2

On notebook paper, write a sentence to demonstrate each of these four kinds of sentences: (1) Declarative, (2) Interrogative, (3) Exclamatory, and (4) Imperative. Write the correct punctuation and the abbreviation that identifies it at the end. Use these abbreviations: **D, Int, E, Imp**.

Chapter 3, Lesson 1, Practice 3: Write *a* or *an* in the blanks.

1. Jack blew out ___ candle.   4. Tim caught ___ fish.   7. ___ poem   10. ___ temple

2. We built ___ tree house.   5. She bruised ___ elbow.   8. ___ bush   11. ___ icicle

3. He dressed up as ___ Eskimo. 6. I want to be ___ actor.   9. ___ armadillo 12. ___ orchard

---

Chapter 3, Lesson 1, Practice 4: Match the definitions. Write the correct letter beside each numbered concept.

_____ 1. expresses strong feeling   A.   verb, adjective, or adverb

_____ 2. makes a statement   B.   noun markers

_____ 3. adjective modifies   C.   person, place, or thing

_____ 4. article adjectives can be called D.   imperative sentence

_____ 5. subject question   E.   declarative sentence

_____ 6. asks a question   F.   exclamatory sentence

_____ 7. makes a request or gives a command G.   interrogative sentence

_____ 8. noun   H.   who or what

_____ 9. tells what the subject does   I.   noun or pronoun

_____ 10. adverb modifies   J.   verb

Chapter 3, Lesson 2, Practice 1: Put the end mark and the abbreviation for each kind of sentence in the blanks below.

1. Sit down when you tie your shoelaces   _____

2. Did you do well on your exam   _____

3. He won every race   _____

4. I'm leaving on my trip tomorrow   _____

5. Cool down after the long race   _____

Chapter 3, Lesson 2, Practice 2

On notebook paper, write a sentence to demonstrate each of these four kinds of sentences: (1) Declarative, (2) Interrogative, (3) Exclamatory, and (4) Imperative. Write the correct punctuation and the abbreviation that identifies it at the end. Use these abbreviations: **D, Int, E, Imp**.

Chapter 3, Lesson 2, Practice 3: Write *a* or *an* in the blanks.

1. I ate ____ fresh strawberry.
2. He is ____ architect.
3. We passed ____ old farm.

4. She wore ____ bonnet.
5. Kate rode ____ elevator.
6. He owns ____ motorcycle.

7. ____ ear
8. ____ nickel
9. ____ emerald

10. ____ pillow
11. ____ bike
12. ____ oval

Chapter 3, Lesson 3, Practice 1: For each noun listed below, write **S** for singular or **P** for plural.

Noun	S or P	Noun	S or P	Noun	S or P
1. houses		4. flights		7. children	
2. gopher		5. calf		8. trees	
3. men		6. building		9. automobile	

Chapter 3, Lesson 3, Practice 2: Write *a* or *an* in the blanks.

1. Did you find ____ penny?
2. Ben was dressed like ____ elf.
3. The zoo had ____ anteater.

4. We explored ____ cave.
5. He plays ____ organ.
6. I chased ____ butterfly.

7. ____ glove
8. ____ helicopter
9. ____ obstacle

10. ____ iron
11. ____ zebra
12. ____ adult

Chapter 3, Lesson 3, Practice 3: Match the definitions. Write the correct letter beside each numbered concept.

_____ 1. tells what the subject does
_____ 2. subject question
_____ 3. adjective modifies
_____ 4. article adjectives can be called
_____ 5. noun
_____ 6. asks a question
_____ 7. makes a request or gives a command
_____ 8. makes a statement
_____ 9. expresses strong feeling
_____ 10. adverb modifies

A. verb, adjective, or adverb
B. noun markers
C. person, place, or thing
D. verb
E. declarative sentence
F. exclamatory sentence
G. interrogative sentence
H. who or what
I. noun or pronoun
J. imperative sentence

Chapter 3, Lesson 3, Practice 4: Put the end mark and the abbreviation for each kind of sentence in the blanks below.

1. Put the books on the shelf _____

2. Do you have any pets _____

3. They discovered the buried treasure _____

4. We will visit Grandma next week _____

Chapter 4, Lesson 1, Practice 1: For each noun listed below, write **C** for common or **P** for proper.

Noun	C or P	Noun	C or P	Noun	C or P	Noun	C or P
1. babies		3. John		5. restaurant		7. truck	
2. German		4. kitten		6. FedEx		8. Ford	

Chapter 4, Lesson 1, Practice 2: Underline the complete subject once and the complete predicate twice.

1. The little puppies growled playfully.
2. Ten large fish swam away.
3. The big yellow bus honked loudly.
4. Four green frogs swam around slowly.

Chapter 4, Lesson 1, Practice 3: Underline the simple subject once and the simple predicate twice.

1. A tiny mouse squeaked.
2. The two yellow cars raced wildly.
3. The vegetable soup cooked slowly.
4. Several children swam yesterday.

Chapter 4, Lesson 1, Practice 4: For each noun listed below, write **S** for singular or **P** for plural.

Noun	S or P	Noun	S or P	Noun	S or P
1. trays		4. women		7. pond	
2. oxen		5. truck		8. wolves	
3. leaves		6. daisy		9. glass	

Chapter 4, Lesson 1, Practice 5: Classify the sentence below. Underline the complete subject once and the complete predicate twice. Then, complete the table below.

_____ The tiny duck waddled slowly away.

List the Noun Used	List the Noun Job	Singular or Plural	Common or Proper	Simple Subject	Simple Predicate

Chapter 4, Lesson 2, Practice 1: Classify the sentence below. Underline the complete subject once and the complete predicate twice. Then, complete the table.

_____ The loud motorcycles thundered quickly away.

List the Noun Used	List the Noun Job	Singular or Plural	Common or Proper	Simple Subject	Simple Predicate

Chapter 4, Lesson 2, Practice 2: Finding One Part of Speech. For each sentence, write **SN** above the simple subject and **V** above the simple predicate. Underline the word(s) for the part of speech listed to the left of each sentence.

Adjective(s):   1. The crisp, crunchy granola crunched loudly.

Adverb(s):   2. The injured gorilla limped very slowly around.

Noun(s):   3. The new book fell open.

Adjective(s):   4. The kittens played outside.

Verb(s):   5. The cougar attacked quickly.

Chapter 4, Lesson 5, Practice Writing Page: Use the two-point outline form below to guide you as you write a two-point expository paragraph.

Write a topic: _____

List 2 points about the topic:

1._____   2._____

Sentence #1	Topic sentence (*Use words in the topic and tell how many points will be used.*)
Sentence #2	2-point sentence (*List your 2 points in the order that you will present them.*)
Sentence #3	State your first point in a complete sentence.
Sentence #4	Write a supporting sentence for the first point.
Sentence #5	State your second point in a complete sentence.
Sentence #6	Write a supporting sentence for the second point.
Sentence #7	Concluding sentence (*Restate the topic sentence and add an extra thought.*)

Student Note: Rewrite your seven-sentence paragraph on notebook paper. Be sure to indent and use the checklists to help you edit your paragraph. Make sure you re-read your paragraph several times, slowly.

Chapter 6, Lesson 1, Practice: For each sentence, do these four things: (1) Write the subject. (2) Write S if the subject is singular or P if the subject is plural. (3) Write the rule number. (4) Underline the correct verb in the sentence.

Rule 1: A singular subject must use a singular verb form that ends in **s**: *is, was, has, does, or verbs ending with* **es**.

Rule 2: A plural subject, a compound subject, or the subject **YOU** must use a plural verb form that has **no s** ending: *are, were, do, have, or verbs without* **s** *or* **es** *endings.* (A plural verb form is also called the *plain form*.)

Subject	S or P	Rule	
			1. The peasants (carries, carry) bags of coffee beans.
			2. Katie and Julia (lives, live) in Peoria now.
			3. During the earthquake, the ground (rumbles, rumble).
			4. She (believe, believes) in miracles.
			5. You (needs, need) to ask for her permission.
			6. Two turtles (stick, sticks) their heads out of the water.
			7. He (reads, read) two books every night.
			8. The dogs (chases, chase) the raccoons through the woods.
			9. James and Lisa (takes, take) turns on the playground.
			10. Jacob quickly (scribble, scribbles) notes onto scrap paper.
			11. The ducks (swim, swims) to the other side of the pond.
			12. Several children (bounce, bounces) happily on the trampoline.

Chapter 6, Lesson 2, Practice: For each sentence, do these four things: (1) Write the subject. (2) Write **S** if the subject is singular or **P** if the subject is plural. (3) Write the rule number. (4) Underline the correct verb in the sentence.

Rule 1: A singular subject must use a singular verb form that ends in **s**: *is, was, has, does, or verbs ending with* **es**.

Rule 2: A plural subject, a compound subject, or the subject **YOU** must use a plural verb form that has **no s** ending: *are, were, do, have, or verbs without* **s** *or* **es** *endings.* (A plural verb form is also called the *plain form.*)

Subject	S or P	Rule	
	P		1. The gnats (swarms, swarm) our picnic table.
			2. Brian and Chris (hikes, hike) up the mountainside.
			3. The rainbow (arches, arch) over the treetops.
			4. My sister (fold, folds) the laundry.
			5. You (watches, watch) your baby sister.
			6. They (takes, take) pictures at the Christmas party.
			7. The new sports car (race, races) quickly down the highway.
			8. The boxes (collapses, collapse) under the heavy weight.
			9. He (passes, pass) the football down the field.
			10. Jenny (begs, beg) her father for permission.

Chapter 6, Lesson 3, Practice: For each sentence, do these four things: (1) Write the subject. (2) Write **S** if the subject is singular or **P** if the subject is plural. (3) Write the rule number. (4) Underline the correct verb in the sentence.

Rule 1: A singular subject must use a singular verb form that ends in **s**: *is, was, has, does, or verbs ending with* **es**.

Rule 2: A plural subject, a compound subject, or the subject **YOU** must use a plural verb form that has **no s** ending: *are, were, do, have, or verbs without* **s** *or* **es** *endings.* (A plural verb form is also called the *plain form.*)

Subject	S or P	Rule	
Sprinklers	P	2	1. The sprinklers (turns, turn) on automatically in the summer.
butterflies	P	2	2. Butterflies (enjoys, enjoy) our flower garden.
address	S	1	3. Her address (changes, change) every six months.
sun	S	1	4. The summer sun (destroy, destroys) the cabbage crops.
You		2	5. You (helps, help) me with my chores.
fingers	P	2	6. My fingers (is, are) blistered.
chef	S	1	7. The new chef (prepares, prepare) seafood salads.
artists	P	2	8. The young artists (paints, paint) a beautiful mural.
Snowflakes	P	2	9. The snowflakes (lands, land) on my tongue.

Chapter 7, Lesson 3, Practice 1

On notebook paper, write seven subject pronouns, seven possessive pronouns, and seven object pronouns.

Chapter 7, Lesson 3, Practice 2

Video tape or tape record all the jingles you have learned.

Chapter 8, Lesson 1, Practice 1

On notebook paper, write seven subject pronouns, seven possessive pronouns, and seven object pronouns.

Chapter 8, Lesson 1, Practice 2: For each sentence, do these four things: (1) Write the subject. (2) Write **S** if the subject is singular or **P** if the subject is plural. (3) Write the rule number. (4) Underline the correct verb in the sentence.

Rule 1: A singular subject must use a singular verb form that ends in **s**: *is, was, has, does, or verbs ending with* **es**.

Rule 2: A plural subject, a compound subject, or the subject **YOU** must use a plural verb form that has **no s** ending: *are, were, do, have, or verbs without* **s** *or* **es** *endings.* (A plural verb form is also called the *plain form.*)

Subject	S or P	Rule	
			1. The children (plays, play) in the sand.
			2. The wind (blows, blow) the trash into the street.
			3. The librarian (ask, asks) my sister to speak softly.
			4. Vines (covers, cover) the willow tree.
			5. You (goes, go) to the amusement park with my family.
			6. Sam and Sarah (walks, walk) through the mall.
			7. She (sleds, sled) down the big hill behind our house.
			8. The chickens (pecks, peck) at the ground.
			9. Bill and Joe (chases, chase) the girls around the yard.
			10. (Was, Were) your money in your pocket?
			11. My brother (slides, slide) into home base.
			12. (Do, Does) the pilots fly every day?

Chapter 8, Lesson 1, Practice 3: Match the definitions. Write the correct letter beside each numbered concept.

_____ 1. subject of an imperative sentence

_____ 2. joins a noun or a pronoun to the rest of the sentence

_____ 3. takes the place of a noun

_____ 4. adjective modifies

_____ 5. noun or pronoun after a preposition

_____ 6. subject question

_____ 7. article adjectives can be called

_____ 8. noun that shows ownership and modifies like an adjective

_____ 9. noun

_____ 10. tells what the subject does

_____ 11. adverb modifies

A. noun markers

B. object of the preposition

C. person, place, or thing

D. possessive noun

E. pronoun

F. preposition

G. you

H. who or what

I. noun or pronoun

J. verb, adjective, or adverb

K. verb

Chapter 8, Lesson 2, Practice: Part A: Underline each noun to be made possessive and write singular or plural (**S-P**), the rule number, and the possessive form. Part B: Write each noun as singular possessive and then as plural possessive.

1. For a singular noun - add (**'s**)		2. For a plural noun that ends in **s** - add (**'**)			3. For a plural noun that does not end in **s** - add (**'s**)		
Rule 1: boy's		**Rule 2: boys'**			**Rule 3: men's**		
Part A	**S-P**	**Rule**	**Possessive Form**		**Part B**	**Singular Poss**	**Plural Poss**
1. sister key					5. bush		
2. elephants peanuts					6. fox		
3. women dresses					7. boss		
4. doctor coat					8. fireman		

Chapter 8, Lesson 3, Practice 1: Number 1-11 on a sheet of paper. Write the answers to the questions listed below.

1. What are the three article adjectives?
2. Name the understood subject pronoun.
3. What is an imperative sentence?
4. What is a declarative sentence?
5. What is an interrogative sentence?
6. What punctuation mark does a possessive noun always have?
7. What part of speech is a possessive noun classified as, and what is the abbreviation used?
8. What is the definition of a pronoun?
9. Name the seven object pronouns.
10. Name the seven subject pronouns.
11. Name the seven possessive pronouns.

Chapter 8, Lesson 3, Practice 2: Part A: Underline each noun to be made possessive and write singular or plural (**S-P**), the rule number, and the possessive form. Part B: Write each noun as singular possessive and then as plural possessive.

1. For a singular noun - add (**'s**)		2. For a plural noun that ends in **s** - add (**'**)		3. For a plural noun that does not end in **s** - add (**'s**)	
Rule 1: boy's		**Rule 2: boys'**		**Rule 3: men's**	

Part A	S-P	Rule	Possessive Form	Part B	Singular Poss	Plural Poss
1. dress hem				5. brother		
2. kittens paws				6. woman		
3. leaves colors				7. puppy		
4. children candy				8. ship		

Chapter 9, Lesson 3, Practice 1: Number 1-11 on a sheet of paper. Write the answers to the questions listed below.

1. What part of speech is the word NOT?
2. Name the understood subject pronoun.
3. What is an imperative sentence?
4. What is a declarative sentence?
5. What is an interrogative sentence?
6. What punctuation mark does a possessive noun always have?
7. What part of speech is a possessive noun classified as, and what is the abbreviation used?
8. List the 8 *be* verbs.
9. What are the parts of a verb phrase?
10. Name the seven subject pronouns.
11. Name the seven possessive pronouns.

Chapter 9, Lesson 3, Practice 2: Part A: Underline each noun to be made possessive and write singular or plural (**S-P**), the rule number, and the possessive form. Part B: Write each noun as singular possessive and as plural possessive.

1. For a singular noun - add (**'s**)		2. For a plural noun that ends in **s** - add (**'**)		3. For a plural noun that does not end in **s** - add (**'s**)	
Rule 1: boy's		**Rule 2: boys'**		**Rule 3: men's**	
Part A	**S-P**	**Rule**	**Possessive Form**	**Part B**	**Singular Poss**	**Plural Poss**

Part A	**S-P**	**Rule**	**Possessive Form**	**Part B**	**Singular Poss**	**Plural Poss**
1. tree height				5. light		
2. rabbits ears				6. baby		
3. quilts threads				7. dolphin		
4. men hair				8. child		

Chapter 10, Lesson 2, Practice: Underline the correct homonym in each sentence.

1. She looked at (their, there) vacation pictures.
2. Joseph (knew, new) about the surprise.
3. He (threw, through) the towel into the basket.
4. The puppy ran (threw, through) the mud.
5. Our team (won, one) the championship game.
6. The (knew, new) stamps were blue and red.
7. We have only (won, one) dollar left.
8. Andrea left the books over (their, there).
9. I wanted another (piece, peace) of pie.
10. Timothy ran (by, buy) the bleachers.
11. She wanted to (by, buy) a new dress.
12. The country prayed for (piece, peace).

Chapter 10, Lesson 3, Practice: Underline the correct homonym in each sentence.

1. We went (through, threw) the lesson together.
2. My brother and I had to (weight, wait) too long.
3. Yesterday, I went (to, two, too) the mall.
4. She couldn't (here, hear) the speaker.
5. Do I (know, no) what you are talking about?
6. There is (know, no) way I am going!
7. The sandpaper was very (coarse, course).
8. My legs felt (week, weak) after the race.
9. The band was on tour for a (week, weak).
10. The golf (course, coarse) was well kept.

Chapter 11, Lesson 3, Practice: Use the Editing Guide below each sentence to know how many capitalization and punctuation errors to correct. For Sentence 1, write the capitalization and punctuation rule numbers for each correction in bold. For Sentence 2, write the capitalization and punctuation corrections. Use the capitalization and punctuation rule pages to help you.

1. **Mr. Lewis,** will you come to our **Christmas** pageant on **Friday, December** 21**?**

   Editing Guide: Capitals: 5   Commas: 2   Periods: 1   End Marks: 1

2. my uncle j b thornton owns a trucking company in west virginia

   Editing Guide: Capitals: 6   Commas: 2   Periods: 2   End Marks: 1

Chapter 12, Lesson 1, Practice: Write the capitalization and punctuation rule number for each correction in bold.

2616 **J**enson **D**rive

Alpino, **A**rizona 75643

August 2, 20—

Dear **A**unt Linda,

   You are so thoughtful**!** **I** appreciate your saving stamps for me for so long. **M**y album is now

complete. **I** have been asked to display it at the local library next month. **T**his is a big honor

for me**.** **I** thought you might like to see it while it's on display**.**

Your devoted nephew,

Tyler

Editing Guide: Capitals: 16   Commas: 4   Apostrophes: 1   End Marks: 6

Chapter 12, Lesson 2, Practice: Write the capitalization and punctuation corrections only.

201 mustang lane

kettle field kentucky 24431

may 19 20—

dear jennifer

we have decided to have some kind of theme at the family reunion this year we

decided to elect a committee to get things going this group of family members would

be in charge of organizing and planning the food music and games for august 4

please contact your uncle phil if you are interested in serving on this special committee

affectionately yours

aunt susan

Editing Guide: Capitals: 18   Commas: 6   End Marks: 4

Chapter 13, Lesson 3, Practice: Find each error and write the correction above it. Write the punctuation corrections where they belong.

Lemons and oranges have miny things in common the most obveous is that they are

both fruits. Both have a tangy flavor, although orangs are sweet. Both fruits has seeds

and grow in trees. Finally, Both need warmer whether to grow and pleanty of sunshine.

Total Mistakes: 12

Chapter 14, Lesson 1, Practice 1: On notebook paper, add the part that is underlined in the parentheses to make each fragment into a complete sentence.

1. In Jeremy's closet   (subject part, predicate part, both the subject and the predicate)

2. Collected and sorted the laundry   (subject part, predicate part, both the subject and the predicate)

3. Three wild turkeys in the yard   (subject part, predicate part, both the subject and the predicate)

Chapter 14, Lesson 1, Practice 2: Identify each kind of sentence by writing the abbreviation in the blank. (S, F)

_____ 1. The wheel turned quickly.

_____ 2. Above the couch in the living room.

_____ 3. The boys sang loudly with the radio.

_____ 4. Watching the television on the floor.

_____ 5. The flag waving from the top of the building.

Chapter 14, Lesson 2, Practice 1: Put a slash to separate each run-on sentence below. Then, correct the run-on sentences by rewriting them as indicated by the labels in parentheses at the end of each sentence.

1. Samantha earned extra money she spent it on makeup. **(SCV)**

_____

2. I am going to the store Jonathan is going to the store. **(SCS)**

_____

3. My little brother is adorable he likes to play games with me. **(SS)**

_____

Chapter 14, Lesson 2, Practice 2: Identify each kind of sentence by writing the abbreviation in the blank. (S, SS, F, SCS, SCV)

_____ 1. Whenever the vegetables are ripe.

_____ 2. My aunt planned the party and invited the guests.

_____ 3. Hot dogs and mustard are good together.

_____ 4. The cat ran away. Dad searched for it.

_____ 5. The pictures were developed in the photo lab.

Chapter 14, Lesson 3, Practice 1: Put a slash to separate each run-on sentence below. Then, correct the run-on sentences by rewriting them as indicated by the labels in parentheses at the end of each sentence.

1. He got lost in the woods he found his way out. **(CD,** but)

   _____

2. He got lost in the woods he found his way out. **(CD,** and)

   _____

3. He got lost in the woods his brother got lost in the woods. **(SCS)**

   _____

4. He got lost in the woods he fell in the pond. **(SCV)**

   _____

Chapter 14, Lesson 3, Practice 2: Identify each kind of sentence by writing the abbreviation in the blank. **(S, F, SCS, SCV, CD)**

_____ 1. The catcher slid and touched the bag.

_____ 2. In the railroad yard on the east end of town.

_____ 3. I like peach pie, but my wife prefers apple pie.

_____ 4. The players and fans were exceptionally angry.

_____ 5. You will stay awake in class, or you will leave.

Chapter 14, Lesson 3, Practice 3

On notebook paper, write two compound sentences using these labels to guide you:

(CD, but) (CD, and)

Chapter 15, Lesson 1, Practice 1: Copy the following words on notebook paper. Write the correct contraction beside each word.

Words: cannot, let us, do not, was not, they are, are not, had not, is not, she is, who is, you are, did not, it is, we are, were not, does not, has not, I am, I have, I had, will not, I will, would not, I would, should not, could not, they would.

Chapter 15, Lesson 1, Practice 2: Put a slash to separate each run-on sentence below. Then, correct the run-on sentences by rewriting them as indicated by the labels in parentheses at the end of each sentence.

1. The dog dug a hole in the ground he buried his bone. (**SCV**)

   _____

2. The dog dug a hole in the ground he buried his bone. (**CD**, and)

   _____

3. The dog chewed on a bone the cat chewed on a bone. (**SCS**)

   _____

Chapter 15, Lesson 1, Practice 3: Identify each kind of sentence by writing the abbreviation in the blank. (**S, F, SCS, SCV, CD**)

_____ 1. The boy tripped and fell on the playground.

_____ 2. Patsy baked the casserole, and Jean set the table.

_____ 3. His mom and dad are in the air force.

_____ 4. Made in factories all across the United States.

_____ 5. I like squash, and my brother likes okra.

Chapter 15, Lesson 2, Practice 1: Copy the following contractions on notebook paper. Write the correct word beside each contraction.

Contractions: can't, let's, don't, wasn't, they're, aren't, hadn't, isn't, she's, who's, you're, didn't, it's, we're, weren't, doesn't, hasn't, I'm, I've, I'd, won't, I'll, wouldn't, shouldn't, couldn't, they'd.

Chapter 15, Lesson 2, Practice 2: Put a slash to separate each run-on sentence below. Then, correct the run-on sentences by rewriting them as indicated by the labels in parentheses at the end of each sentence.

1. The robins gathered twigs they built a nest. (**SCV**)

   _____

2. The robins gathered twigs they searched for worms also. (**CD**, but)

   _____

3. The robins searched for worms the chickens searched for worms. (**SCS**)

   _____

Chapter 15, Lesson 2, Practice 3: Identify each kind of sentence by writing the abbreviation in the blank. (**S, F, SCS, SCV, CD**)

_____ 1. The actors danced and sang during the musical.

_____ 2. Travis watched the children, and Donna went to the mall.

_____ 3. My aunt and uncle are missionaries in Russia.

_____ 4. Moved to the north side of the city.

_____ 5. He likes to vacuum, and she likes to dust the furniture.

Chapter 15, Lesson 3, Practice 1: Copy the following words on another sheet of paper. Write the correct contraction beside each word.

Words: I am, he is, it is, that is, there is, you are, they are, were not, does not, cannot, has not, she has, have not, you have, they have, I would, he had, you had, they had, I will, she will, we will, we would, should not, could not.

Chapter 15, Lesson 3, Practice 2: Put a slash to separate each run-on sentence below. Then, correct the run-on sentences by rewriting them as indicated by the labels in parentheses at the end of each sentence.

1. Tyler tripped on the power cord he bruised both of his knees. (**SCV**)

   _____

2. Tyler tripped on the power cord he didn't turn over the television. (**CD, but**)

   _____

3. Tyler tripped on the power cord Ginger tripped on the power cord. (**SCS**)

   _____

Chapter 15, Lesson 3, Practice 3: Identify each kind of sentence by writing the abbreviation in the blank. (**S, F, SCS, SCV, CD**)

_____ 1. The raccoon ducked and dodged the highway traffic.

_____ 2. Jeremy raked the leaves, and Henry mowed the lawn.

_____ 3. Julie's brother and sister are twins.

_____ 4. Watched as the clouds floated by.

_____ 5. I like chocolate, and Rebecca likes vanilla.

Chapter 16, Lesson 1, Practice 1: Underline each subject and fill in each column according to the title.

	List each Verb	Write PrN, PA, or None	Write L or A
1. Those lemons are sour.			
2. My new car is beautiful.			
3. They listened to the presenter.			
4. Tigers are fierce creatures.			
5. She is our new mayor.			
6. All the dishes are dirty.			
7. That song was very popular.			
8. Sally marched in the parade.			
9. They visited the new stadium.			
10. Patrick is a good athlete.			
11. My sister is mowing the lawn.			
12. Denver is a very large city.			
13. The river was beautiful.			
14. Kelly is the youngest child.			
15. Oliver is my pet iguana.			

Chapter 16, Lesson 1, Practice 2: Copy the following words on another sheet of paper. Write the correct contraction beside each word.

<u>Words:</u> Should not, they will, will not, we had, have not, I have, she is, let us, cannot, do not, we are, what is, it is, is not, I am.

Chapter 16, Lesson 2, Practice 1: Tell whether each sentence is an example of a simile or a metaphor by writing *like* or *as* in the Simile column or by writing the noun in the predicate that renames the subject in the Metaphor column.

	Simile	Metaphor
1. My stomach fluttered like butterflies.		
2. The strong linebacker was a bulldozer.		
3. Her voice was as sweet as sugar.		
4. The young American swimmer was a fish.		
5. We were so hungry that we ate like pigs.		

Chapter 16, Lesson 2, Practice 2: Underline each subject and fill in each column according to the title.

	List each Verb	Write PrN, PA, or None	Write L or A
1. My brother rode his bike to town.			
2. Her essay was exciting.			
3. My mother is an artist.			
4. Samantha is my cousin.			
5. The autumn leaves are yellow.			
6. My brother sold his guitar.			
7. We went to the mall yesterday.			

Chapter 16, Lesson 2, Practice 3: Copy the following contractions on notebook paper. Write the correct word beside each contraction.

Contractions: hasn't, he's, I've, they've, she'd, won't, she'll, you'll, couldn't, let's, can't, doesn't, don't, weren't, you're, there's, what's, who's, isn't, I'm.

Chapter 16, Lesson 3, Practice 1: Copy the following words on notebook paper. Write the correct contraction beside each word.

Words: let us, does not, do not, was not, are not, there is, that is, it is, is not, should not, would not, you would, they had, had not, they have, have not, has not, he has, you are, who is.

Chapter 16, Lesson 3, Practice 2: Tell whether each sentence is an example of a simile or a metaphor by writing *like* or *as* in the Simile column or by writing the noun in the predicate that renames the subject in the Metaphor column.

	Simile	Metaphor
1. Kindness is the fruit of human understanding.		
2. His patience wore as thin as gift wrap.		
3. The storm clouds came like a thief in the night.		
4. My neighbor's baby is a little angel.		
5. The climber scaled the slope like a mountain goat.		

Chapter 16, Lesson 3, Practice 3: Underline each subject and fill in each column according to the title.

	List each Verb	Write PrN, PA, or None	Write L or A
1. The vegetables are fresh.			
2. His hometown is small.			
3. They passed by the new shops.			
4. Bats are my favorite animal.			
5. He is my youngest brother.			
6. Some of the pieces are missing.			
7. I watched my favorite movie.			

Chapter 17, Lesson 1, Practice: Use the Quotation Rules to help punctuate the quotations below. Underline the explanatory words.

1. ms smith said thank you for your help

2. thank you for your help ms smith said

3. after football practice i gasped mom im starving

4. mom im starving i gasped after football practice

5. pastor thomas replied the church picnic will be next sunday

6. the church picnic will be next sunday pastor thomas replied

7. i screamed during the scary movie look out

8. look out i screamed during the scary movie

Chapter 17, Lesson 2, Practice 1: Tell whether each sentence is an example of a simile or a metaphor by writing *like* or *as* in the Simile column or by writing the noun in the predicate that renames the subject in the Metaphor column.

	Simile	Metaphor
1. The frightened horse ran like a bolt of lightning.		
2. The sun was a blazing round ball.		
3. Our goat is as tame as a kitten.		

Chapter 17, Lesson 2, Practice 2: Copy the following words on another sheet of paper. Write the correct contraction beside each word.

Words: cannot, let us, do not, was not, they are, are not, had not, is not, she is, who is, you are, did not, it is, we are, were not, does not, has not, I am, I have, I had, will not, I will, would not, should not, could not, they would.

Chapter 17, Lesson 2, Practice 3: Underline each subject and fill in each column according to the title.

	List each Verb	Write PrN, PA, or None	Write L or A
1. My brother ate forty marshmallows.			
2. That movie is funny.			
3. Those flowers are roses.			
4. Her dress is pretty.			
5. He is our new pastor.			

Chapter 17, Lesson 2, Practice 4: Use the Quotation Rules to help punctuate the quotations below. Underline the explanatory words.

1. the patient asked why does my head hurt

2. why does my head hurt asked the patient

3. dad yelled theres a cow in our pool

4. will you go to the park with me james asked

5. you can have an apple before dinner mother replied

6. daniel said i wrote a poem for mrs clark

Chapter 17, Lesson 3, Practice 1: Use the Quotation Rules to help punctuate the quotations below. Underline the explanatory words.

1. i have no doubt you will enjoy hearing the trinity choir in concert said mr lawrence

2. mr lawrence said i have no doubt you will enjoy hearing the trinity choir in concert

3. will you visit aunt betty in boise idaho this fall asked heather

4. heather asked will you visit aunt betty in boise idaho this fall

5. susan stated i didnt know that mrs peterson wore glasses

Chapter 17, Lesson 3, Practice 2

On notebook paper, write a sentence demonstrating a beginning quote and a sentence demonstrating an end quote.

Chapter 17, Lesson 3, Practice 3

On notebook paper, write one sentence for each of these labels: **(SCS) (SCV) (CD)**.

Chapter 18, Lesson 1, Practice: Identify each verb as regular or irregular by writing **R** or **I** in the first blank and the past tense form in the second blank. Also, underline each verb or verb phrase in Sentences 6-10.

Verb	R or I	Past Tense	Underline the Verb	R or I	Past Tense
1. come			6. Heidi gives instructions to Phil.		
2. push			7. Dawn reached for her purse.		
3. prove			8. Margie is sitting in the corner.		
4. write			9. Turner wrote the article.		
5. blow			10. Dana likes her baby cousin.		

Chapter 18, Lesson 2, Practice: Underline each verb or verb phrase. Identify the verb tense by writing a number **1** for present tense, a number **2** for past tense, or a number **3** for future tense. Write the past tense form and **R** or **I** for Regular or Irregular.

Verb Tense		Main Verb Past Tense Form	R or I
	1. Those acorns did fall from our tree.		
	2. That ship is sailing tomorrow.		
	3. They are eating pizza in the lunchroom.		
	4. Tonight, I will clean my room.		
	5. Mary does work at the local hospital.		
	6. Doug will wear purple shoes to school.		
	7. Kevin had sold all his candy.		
	8. Mom was exercising at the gym.		
	9. I have grown three inches.		
	10. I will work for Mr. Green next week.		

Chapter 18, Lesson 3, Practice 1: Underline each verb or verb phrase. Identify the verb tense by writing a number **1** for present tense, a number **2** for past tense, or a number **3** for future tense. Write the past tense form and **R** or **I** for Regular or Irregular.

Verb Tense		Main Verb Past Tense Form	R or I
	1. I did ride the brown and white pony.		
	2. Shall I bring money for the trip?		
	3. Beth will grade papers for Ms. Cook.		
	4. I am decorating cupcakes for the party.		

Chapter 18, Lesson 3, Practice 2: Change the underlined present tense verbs in Paragraph 1 to past tense verbs in Paragraph 2.

Paragraph 1: Present Tense

My family **is** well organized for camping trips. Mom **plans** the meals and **packs** the food. I **gather** and **load** the camping gear. My dad **locates** the fishing gear and **places** it in the boat. He **checks** all the supplies carefully. We never **leave** for a camping trip without the necessary food and gear!

Paragraph 2: Past Tense

My family _____ well organized for camping trips. Mom _____ the meals and

_____ the food. I _____ and _____ the

camping gear. My dad_____ the fishing gear and _____ it in the

boat. He _____ all the supplies carefully. We never _____ for a

camping trip without the necessary food and gear!

Chapter 18, Lesson 3, Practice 3

On notebook paper, write the seven present tense helping verbs, the five past tense helping verbs, and the two future tense helping verbs.

Chapter 18, Lesson 3, Practice 4: Change the underlined mixed tense verbs in Paragraph 1 to present tense verbs in Paragraph 2.

Paragraph 1: Mixed Tenses

My family **ate** dinner at Grandmother's house every Sunday. She always **cooks** a gigantic feast! Grandmother **fried** chicken in a big black skillet. It always **looks** and **smelled** delicious! Her vegetables often **tasted** fresh from the vine. Grandmother also **baked** fresh bread and pastries. Sunday afternoons at Grandmother's house **are filled** with love, food, and family.

Paragraph 2: Present Tense

My family _____ dinner at Grandmother's house every Sunday. She always _____ a

gigantic feast! Grandmother _____ chicken in a big black skillet. It always

_____ and _____ delicious! Her vegetables often _____

fresh from the vine. Grandmother also _____ fresh bread and pastries. Sunday

afternoons at Grandmother's house _____ _____ with love, food, and family.

Chapter 19, Lesson 1, Practice 1: Underline the negative words in each sentence. Rewrite each sentence on notebook paper and correct the double negative mistake as indicated by the rule number in parentheses at the end of the sentence.

Rule 1	Rule 2	Rule 3
Change the second negative to a positive.	Take out the negative part of a contraction.	Remove the first negative word (verb change).

1. Danny doesn't have no money. (Rule 3)
2. Our old truck doesn't never start. (Rule 1)
3. Maria wouldn't never say that. (Rule 2)
4. The hunters didn't have no license. (Rule 1)
5. Our house doesn't have no shutters. (Rule 3)
6. The volunteers didn't want no pay. (Rule 3)
7. He wouldn't do no wrong. (Rule 2)
8. There isn't no milk in the refrigerator. (Rule 1)

Chapter 19, Lesson 1, Practice 2: Underline each verb or verb phrase. Identify the verb tense by writing a number **1** for present tense, a number **2** for past tense, or a number **3** for future tense. Write the past tense form and **R** or **I** for Regular or Irregular.

Verb Tense		Main Verb Past Tense Form	R or I
	1. He is swimming in deep water.		
	2. Will he search for the lost diamond?		
	3. Jody ate her dessert first.		
	4. Has he signed the checks yet?		
	5. Did he shoot the wild pheasant?		

Chapter 19, Lesson 2, Practice 1: Underline the negative words in each sentence. Rewrite each sentence on notebook paper and correct the double negative mistake as indicated by the rule number in parentheses at the end of the sentence.

Rule 1	Rule 2	Rule 3
Change the second negative to a positive.	Take out the negative part of a contraction.	Remove the first negative word (verb change).

1. He didn't believe nothing I said. (Rule 1)
2. Don't never pay with cash. (Rule 1)
3. I wouldn't never eat spinach. (Rule 2)
4. Mark hadn't never owned a dog. (Rule 2)
5. The fisherman didn't catch no fish. (Rule 3)
6. We didn't find no arrowheads in the cave. (Rule 3)
7. She couldn't find nothing she liked. (Rule 1)
8. We haven't received no payment. (Rule 2)

Chapter 19, Lesson 2, Practice 2: Underline each verb or verb phrase. Identify the verb tense by writing a number **1** for present tense, a number **2** for past tense, or a number **3** for future tense. Write the past tense form and **R** or **I** for Regular or Irregular.

Verb Tense		Past Tense	R or I
	1. We will be staying in Des Moines.		
	2. Did he really win the jackpot?		
	3. He fell from the edge of the cliff.		
	4. Chris is studying for his algebra test.		

Chapter 19, Lesson 2, Practice 3: Change the underlined present tense verbs in Paragraph 1 to past tense verbs in Paragraph 2.

Paragraph 1: Present Tense

Paul **delivers** newspapers after school. He **wants** to earn enough money for summer camp. He **has** a route that **covers** ten city blocks. He always **throws** the papers on the driveway, and his faithful customers **think** he **does** a great job.

Paragraph 2: Past Tense

Paul _____ newspapers after school. He _____ to earn

enough money for summer camp. He _____ a route that _____ ten

city blocks. He always _____ the papers on the driveway, and his faithful

customers _____ he _____ a great job.

Chapter 19, Lesson 2, Practice 4

On notebook paper, write the seven present tense helping verbs, the five past tense helping verbs, and the two future tense helping verbs.

Chapter 19, Lesson 3, Practice 1: Copy the following words on notebook paper. Write the correct contraction beside each word.

Words: cannot, let us, do not, was not, they are, are not, had not, is not, she is, who is, you are, did not, it is, we are, were not, does not.

Chapter 19, Lesson 3, Practice 2: Underline the negative words in each sentence. Rewrite each sentence on notebook paper and correct the double negative mistake as indicated by the rule number in parentheses at the end of the sentence.

Rule 1	Rule 2	Rule 3
Change the second negative to a positive.	Take out the negative part of a contraction.	Remove the first negative word (verb change).

1. He didn't want nothing in return. (Rule 3)
2. I don't have no fever today. (Rule 1)
3. She can't never find her glasses. (Rule 2)
4. Gary doesn't have no brothers. (Rule 1)
5. Don't never leave your car unlocked. (Rule 1)
6. There wasn't no dessert left. (Rule 2)

Chapter 19, Lesson 3, Practice 3: Change the underlined mixed tense verbs in Paragraph 1 to present tense verbs in Paragraph 2.

Paragraph 1: Mixed Tenses

Jill **grabs** her blanket out of the car and **climbed** up the steps to the stadium. She **bought** her ticket at the ticket booth and **walks** through the gate. She **found** a seat in the bleachers next to her friends and **spreads** out her blanket. Soon, the game **begins**, and she **cheers** for the home team.

Paragraph 2: Present Tense

Jill _____ her blanket out of the car and _____ up the steps to the stadium. She _____ her ticket at the ticket booth and _____ through the gate. She _____ a seat in the bleachers next to her friends and _____ out her blanket. Soon, the game_____, and she _____ for the home team.

Chapter 20, Lesson 1, Practice 1: Write the rule number from Reference 60 and the correct plural form of the nouns below.

		Rule	Plural Form			Rule	Plural Form
1.	day			6.	match		
2.	knife			7.	patio		
3.	puff			8.	tomato		
4.	deer			9.	star		
5.	man			10.	spy		

Chapter 20, Lesson 1, Practice 2

On notebook paper, write the seven present tense helping verbs, the five past tense helping verbs, and the two future tense helping verbs.

Chapter 20, Lesson 2, Practice 1: Write the rule number from Reference 60 and the correct plural form of the nouns below.

	Rule	Plural Form			Rule	Plural Form
1. journey				6. church		
2. leaf				7. video		
3. gulf				8. volcano		
4. sheep				9. car		
5. mouse				10. party		

Chapter 20, Lesson 2, Practice 2: Underline the negative words in each sentence. Rewrite each sentence on notebook paper and correct the double negative mistake as indicated by the rule number in parentheses at the end of the sentence.

Rule 1	Rule 2	Rule 3
Change the second negative to a positive.	Take out the negative part of a contraction.	Remove the first negative word (verb change).

1. There wasn't no cake left. (Rule 1)

2. Lucy doesn't have no paper. (Rule 3)

3. We don't see nothing on the table. (Rule 1)

4. Mike hadn't never bought a new car. (Rule 2)

5. They didn't see nothing in the barn. (Rule 2)

6. Don't never stay home alone. (Rule 1)

Chapter 20, Lesson 3, Practice 1: Underline each subject and fill in each column according to the title.

	List each Verb	Write PrN, PA, or None	Write L or A
1. Paris is a beautiful city.			
2. He worked on the car.			
3. The papers are graded.			
4. The dog barked during the night.			
5. Those two girls are sisters.			
6. My feet are sore.			

Chapter 20, Lesson 3, Practice 2: Write the rule number from Reference 60 and the correct plural form of the nouns below.

	Rule	Plural Form			Rule	Plural Form
1. alloy				6. kiss		
2. shelf				7. rodeo		
3. roof				8. dingo		
4. moose				9. dinosaur		
5. fireman				10. pastry		

Chapter 20, Lesson 3, Practice 3: Underline the negative words in each sentence. Rewrite each sentence on notebook paper and correct the double negative mistake as indicated by the rule number in parentheses at the end of the sentence.

Rule 1	Rule 2	Rule 3
Change the second negative to a positive.	Take out the negative part of a contraction.	Remove the first negative word (verb change).

1. The boys didn't ride no roller coaster. (Rule 3)

2. We hadn't never been to a football game. (Rule 2)

3. She doesn't want no candy. (Rule 1)

4. She didn't see nothing to buy. (Rule 1)

Chapter 20, Lesson 3, Practice 4: Underline each verb or verb phrase. Identify the verb tense by writing a number **1** for present tense, a number **2** for past tense, or a number **3** for future tense. Write the past tense form and **R** or **I** for Regular or Irregular.

Verb Tense		Main Verb Past Tense Form	R or I
	1. Did you write that poem?		
	2. Betty will watch the children.		
	3. Tomorrow, he will drive to school.		
	4. I worked with a new boss.		

Chapter 20, Lesson 3, Practice 5: Copy the following words on notebook paper. Write the correct contraction beside each word.

Words: cannot, let us, do not, was not, they are, are not, had not, is not, she is, who is, you are, did not, it is, we are, were not, does not.

Chapter 21, Lesson 1, Practice

Use butcher paper, large pieces of construction paper, or poster board to make a colorful wall poster identifying the five parts of a friendly letter and the parts of an envelope. Write the title and an example for each of the five parts. Illustrate your work. Then, give an oral presentation about the friendly letter and the envelope when you have finished.

Chapter 21, Lesson 2, Practice

Write a friendly letter to a special friend or relative. Before you start, review the references and tips for writing friendly letters. After your letter has been edited, fold the letter and put it in an envelope. Address the envelope properly and mail it. Don't forget the stamp.

Chapter 21, Lesson 3, Practice 1

On notebook paper, identify the parts of a friendly letter and envelope by writing the titles and an example for each title. Use References 63 and 64 to help you.

Chapter 21, Lesson 3, Practice 2

Write a friendly letter to a neighbor, nursing home resident, or relative. This person must be someone different from the person chosen in the previous lesson. Before you start, review the references and tips for writing friendly letters. After your letter has been edited, fold the letter and put it in an envelope. Address the envelope properly and mail it. Don't forget the stamp.

Chapter 22, Lesson 1, Practice

Use butcher paper, large pieces of construction paper, or poster board to make a colorful wall poster identifying the six parts of a business letter and the parts of a business envelope. Write the title and an example for each of the six parts of the business letter and envelope. Illustrate your work. Then, give an oral presentation about the business letter and the envelope when you have finished.

Chapter 22, Lesson 2, Practice 1

Write a friendly letter to a special friend or relative. Before you start, review the references and tips for writing friendly letters. After your letter has been edited, fold the letter and put it in an envelope. Address the envelope properly and mail it. Don't forget the stamp.

Chapter 22, Lesson 2, Practice 2

Write a business letter. You may invent the company and the situation for which you are writing. Before you begin, review the reasons for writing business letters and the four types of business letters (*Reference 65 on page 50*). After your letter has been edited, fold the letter and put it in an envelope. Address the envelope properly.

Chapter 22, Lesson 3, Practice

Choose a city that you would like to visit. Write several letters requesting information about the city you have chosen. (*You may need to research the different places to send the letters.*) Next, you are to use encyclopedias, newspapers, magazines, and even the Internet to find out about the interesting sites that you would like to see in your chosen city.

Chapter 23, Lesson 1, Practice

Write your own thank-you note. First, think of a person who has done something nice for you or has given you a gift (even the gift of time). Next, write that person a thank-you note, using the information in the Reference Section as a guide.

Chapter 23, Lesson 2, Practice 1: Match each part of a book listed below with the type of information it may give you. Write the appropriate letter in the blank. You may use each letter only once.

A. Body	B. Preface	C. Bibliography	D. Index	E. Copyright page	F. Appendix

_____ 1. Exact page numbers for a particular topic and used to locate topics quickly

_____ 2. Text of the book

_____ 3. Reason the book was written

_____ 4. Books listed for finding more information

_____ 5. ISBN number

_____ 6. Extra maps in a book

Chapter 23, Lesson 2, Practice 2

Write the nine parts of a book on a poster and write a description beside each part. Illustrate and color the nine parts.

Chapter 23, Lesson 3, Practice: Underline the correct answers.

1. The main reference book that is primarily a book of maps is the
   (encyclopedia   dictionary   atlas   almanac).

2. What would you find by going to *The Readers' Guide to Periodical Literature*?
   (newspaper articles   magazine articles   encyclopedia articles)

3. Fiction books contain information and stories that are   (true   not true).

4. The main reference book that is published once a year with a variety of up-to-date
   information is the   (encyclopedia   dictionary   atlas   almanac).

5. The main reference book that gives the definition, spelling, and pronunciation of words is the
   (encyclopedia   dictionary   atlas   almanac).

6. Nonfiction books contain information and stories that are   (true   not true).

Chapter 24, Lesson 1, Practice: Put each group of words in alphabetical order. Write numbers in the blanks to show the order in each column.

School Words	Birthday Words	"C" Words	Garden Words	"P" Words
____ 1. recess	____ 7. cake	____ 13. cave	____ 19. plant	____ 25. paddle
____ 2. teacher	____ 8. candles	____ 14. cymbal	____ 20. fertilizer	____ 26. penny
____ 3. student	____ 9. balloons	____ 15. channel	____ 21. seeds	____ 27. powder
____ 4. homework	____ 10. party	____ 16. cigar	____ 22. weeds	____ 28. paint
____ 5. books	____ 11. presents	____ 17. cross	____ 23. hoe	____ 29. pioneer
____ 6. test	____ 12. games	____ 18. cricket	____ 24. water	____ 30. pipe

---

Chapter 24, Lesson 2, Practice : Below are the tops of two dictionary pages. Write the page number on which each word listed would appear.

freighter (first word)	Page 300	friendly (last word)	friendship (first word)	Page 301	front (last word)
Page		**Page**	**Page**		**Page**
_____ 1. fright		_____ 3. fringe	_____ 5. friction		_____ 7. frisky
_____ 2. fried		_____ 4. frog	_____ 6. from		_____ 8. fresh

Chapter 24, Lesson 3, Practice 1: Match the definitions of the parts of a dictionary entry below. Write the correct letter of the word beside each definition.

_____ 1. small *n.* for noun, small *v.* for verb, *adj.* for adjective, etc.

_____ 2. sentences using the entry word to illustrate a meaning

_____ 3. words that have similar meanings to the entry word

_____ 4. shows how to pronounce a word, usually put in parentheses

_____ 5. correct spelling and divides the word into syllables

_____ 6. numbered definitions listed according to the part of speech

A. pronunciation

B. meanings

C. entry word

D. synonyms

E. parts of speech

F. examples

Chapter 24, Lesson 3, Practice 2: Label each part of the dictionary entry below. Use the definitions in the matching exercise to help you.

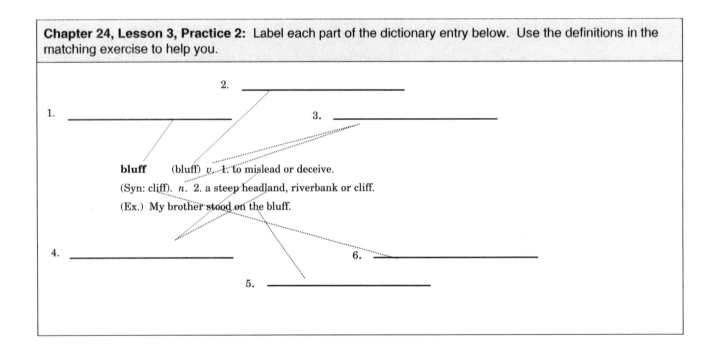

TEST

SECTION

Chapter 1 Test

Exercise 1: Identify each pair of words as synonyms or antonyms by putting parentheses ( ) around **syn** or **ant**. For number 5, write two synonym words and identify them with **syn**. For number 6, write two antonym words and identify them with **ant**.

1. often, seldom	syn ant	3. master, servant	syn ant	5.
2. friendly, amiable	syn ant	4. small, minute	syn ant	6.

Exercise 2: Write **a** or **an** in the blanks.

1. We rode ____ train.
2. I saw ____ eagle.
3. Monday is ____ holiday.
4. He found ____ empty bottle.
5. It was ____ easy test.
6. He is ____ good friend.
7. ___ acorn
8. ___ telephone
9. ___ otter
10. ___ hat
11. ___ oven
12. ___ ring

Exercise 3: In your journal, write a paragraph summarizing what you have learned this week.

Chapter 2 Test

Exercise 1: Identify each pair of words as synonyms or antonyms by putting parentheses ( ) around **syn** or **ant**.

1. small, minute	syn ant	3. servant, master	syn ant	5. apt, suitable	syn ant
2. clear, vague	syn ant	4. doubtful, certain	syn ant	6. weary, tired	syn ant

Exercise 2: Write **a** or **an** in the blanks.

1. We saw ___ clown today.
2. It was ___ amazing idea.
3. We have ___ unusual house.
4. It is ___ clever trick.
5. It was ___ easy job.
6. We want ___ new car.
7. ___ ostrich
8. ___ siren
9. ___ estimate
10. ___ gnu
11. ___ elf
12. ___ book

Exercise 3: Match the definitions. Write the correct letter beside each numbered concept.

_____ 1. sentences should begin with
_____ 2. article adjectives
_____ 3. adjective modifies
_____ 4. verb question
_____ 5. tells what the subject does
_____ 6. subject-noun question (thing)
_____ 7. article adjective can be called
_____ 8. parts of a complete sentence
_____ 9. noun
_____ 10. subject-noun question (person)
_____ 11. adverb modifies

A. verb, adjective, or adverb
B. who
C. what is being said about
D. person, place, or thing
E. what
F. a capital letter
G. subject, verb, complete sense
H. a, an, the
I. noun or pronoun
J. verb
K. noun marker

Exercise 4: In your journal, write a paragraph summarizing what you have learned this week.

Chapter 3 Test

Exercise 1: Classify each sentence.

1. _____ An inactive volcano erupted quite unexpectedly!

2. _____ The very bright Christmas lights blinked rather slowly.

Exercise 2: Identify each pair of words as synonyms or antonyms by putting parentheses ( ) around **syn** or **ant**.

1. sever, cut	(syn) ant	4. apt, suitable	syn ant	7. curiosity, interest	(syn) ant
2. vague, clear	syn ant	5. tasty, bland	syn ant	8. friendly, amiable	(syn) ant
3. weary, tired	(syn) ant	6. seldom, often	syn (ant)	9. kind, irreverent	syn (ant)

Exercise 3: Put the end marks and the abbreviations for each kind of sentence in the blanks below.

1. Did you vote in the election   _____

2. My uncle bought a new car   _____

3. I lost my new job   _____

4. Turn the heat on low   _____

Exercise 4: Write **a** or **an** in the blanks.

1. We rode ____ elk.   3. Did you see ____ elf?   5. ____ plate   7. ____ ant

2. He was ____ funny juggler.   4. I have ____ banjo.   6. ____ chimney   8. ____ ape

Exercise 5: For each noun listed below, write **S** for singular or **P** for plural.

Noun	S or P	Noun	S or P	Noun	S or P
1. books		4. children		7. shelves	
2. door		5. planet		8. men	
3. roads		6. star		9. car	

Exercise 6: Match the definitions. Write the correct letter beside each numbered concept.

_____ 1. tells what the subject does   A. verb, adjective, or adverb
_____ 2. article adjectives   B. who or what
_____ 3. adjective modifies   C. what is being said about
_____ 4. verb question   D. person, place, or thing
_____ 5. subject-noun question   E. a, an, the
_____ 6. noun   F. noun or pronoun
_____ 7. adverb modifies   G. verb

Exercise 7: On notebook paper, write the four kinds of sentences: Declarative, Interrogative, Exclamatory, and Imperative. Write the correct punctuation and the abbreviation that identifies it at the end. Use these abbreviations: **D, Int, E, Imp.**

Exercise 8: In your journal, write a paragraph summarizing what you have learned this week.

Chapter 4 Test

Exercise 1: Classify each sentence.

1. _____ The professional baseball player pitched wildly today!

2. _____ Two feisty lion cubs played vigorously together.

3. _____ An exceptionally strong wind blew fiercely yesterday.

Exercise 2: Use Sentence 2 to underline the complete subject once and the complete predicate twice and to complete the table below.

List the Noun Used	List the Noun Job	Singular or Plural	Common or Proper	Simple Subject	Simple Predicate
1.	2.	3.	4.	5.	6.

Exercise 3: Name the four parts of speech that you have studied. (*You may use abbreviations.*)

1. _____   2. _____   3. _____   4. _____

Exercise 4: Identify each pair of words as synonyms or antonyms by putting parentheses ( ) around *syn* or *ant*.

1. small, minute	syn ant	5. pillar, column	syn ant	9. apt, suitable	syn ant
2. master, servant	syn ant	6. soiled, clean	syn ant	10. curiosity, interest	syn ant
3. vague, clear	syn ant	7. sever, cut	syn ant	11. doubtful, certain	syn ant
4. attempt, try	syn ant	8. seldom, often	syn ant	12. eager, indifferent	syn ant

Exercise 5: For each noun listed below, write **S** for singular or **P** for plural.

Noun	S or P	Noun	S or P	Noun	S or P	Noun	S or P
1. trail		3. feet		5. playground		7. butterfly	
2. pencils		4. puppies		6. mice		8. alleys	

Exercise 6: For each noun listed below, write **C** for common or **P** for proper.

Noun	C or P	Noun	C or P	Noun	C or P	Noun	C or P
1. teacher		3. American		5. lamp		7. bicycle	
2. Patsy		4. sky		6. Taco Bell		8. Honda	

Exercise 7: Underline the complete subject once and the complete predicate twice.
1. The two boys wrestled carelessly.   3. The little brown bug scurried quickly.
2. Ten large birds flew away.   4. Four lanky runners ran briskly.

Exercise 8: Underline the simple subject once and the simple predicate twice.
1. A tiny baby cried.   3. The chicken soup boiled wildly.
2. The two yellow flowers wilted today.   4. Several bees swarmed yesterday.

Exercise 9: On notebook paper, write a Practice Sentence and an Improved Sentence. Use these labels:
A Adj Adj SN V Adv.

Exercise 10: In your journal, write a paragraph summarizing what you have learned this week.

Chapter 5 Test

Exercise 1: Classify each sentence.

1. _____ Martha sang beautifully in front of a large audience yesterday.

2. _____ The lively ponies ran gracefully through the field toward the barn.

3. _____ An old man sat peacefully on the park bench during the early morning.

Exercise 2: Use Sentence 1 to underline the complete subject once and the complete predicate twice and to complete the table below.

List the Noun Used	List the Noun Job	Singular or Plural	Common or Proper	Simple Subject	Simple Predicate
1.	2.	3.	4.	5.	6.
7.	8.	9.	10.		
11.	12.	13.	14.		

Exercise 3: Name the five parts of speech that you have studied. (*You may use abbreviations.*)

1. _____   2. _____   3. _____   4. _____   5. _____

Exercise 4: Identify each pair of words as synonyms or antonyms by putting parentheses ( ) around **syn** or **ant**.

1. attempt, try	syn ant	5. interest, curiosity	syn ant	9. amiable, friendly	syn ant
2. tasty, bland	syn ant	6. doubtful, certain	syn ant	10. pillar, column	syn ant
3. watch, vigil	syn ant	7. deadly, lethal	syn ant	11. flabby, firm	syn ant
4. sever, cut	syn ant	8. cheap, costly	syn ant	12. eager, indifferent	syn ant

Exercise 5: Match the definitions. Write the correct letter beside each numbered concept.

_____ 1. joins a noun or a pronoun to the rest of the sentence
_____ 2. makes a statement
_____ 3. adjective modifies
_____ 4. noun or pronoun after a preposition
_____ 5. subject questions
_____ 6. article adjectives can be called
_____ 7. makes a request or gives a command
_____ 8. noun
_____ 9. tells what the subject does
_____ 10. adverb modifies

A. verb, adjective, or adverb
B. object of the preposition
C. person, place, or thing
D. imperative sentence
E. declarative sentence
F. preposition
G. noun markers
H. who or what
I. noun or pronoun
J. verb

Exercise 6: On notebook paper, write as many prepositions as you can.

Exercise 7: In your journal, write a paragraph summarizing what you have learned this week.

Chapter 6 Test

Exercise 1: Classify each sentence.

1. _____ The young pioneer children rode to school on horseback.

2. _____ Many strange creatures live in the depths of the sea.

3. _____ The extremely light arrow flew straight for the center of the target!

Exercise 2: Use Sentence 3 to underline the complete subject once and the complete predicate twice and to complete the table below.

List the Noun Used	List the Noun Job	Singular or Plural	Common or Proper	Simple Subject	Simple Predicate
1.	2.	3.	4.	5.	6.
7.	8.	9.	10.		
11.	12.	13.	14.		

Exercise 3: Name the five parts of speech that you have studied. (*You may use abbreviations.*)

1. _____ 2. _____ 3. _____ 4. _____ 5. _____

Exercise 4: Identify each pair of words as synonyms or antonyms by putting parentheses ( ) around **syn** or **ant**.

1. weary, tired	syn ant	5. soiled, clean	syn ant	9. lethal, deadly	(syn) ant
2. present, absent	syn ant	6. firm, flabby	syn ant	10. burst, explode	syn ant
3. friendly, amiable	syn (ant)	7. chicken, fowl	syn ant	11. cheap, costly	syn ant
4. vigil, watch	syn ant	8. receive, send	syn (ant)	12. kind, irreverent	syn ant

Exercise 5: For each sentence, do these four things: (1) Write the subject. (2) Write **S** if the subject is singular or **P** if the subject is plural. (3) Write the rule number. (4) Underline the correct verb in the sentence.

> Rule 1: A singular subject must use a singular verb form that ends in **s**: *is, was, has, does, or verbs ending with* **es**.
>
> Rule 2: A plural subject, a compound subject, or the subject **YOU** must use a plural verb form that has **no s** ending: *are, were, do, have, or verbs without* **s** *or* **es** *endings.* (A plural verb form is also called the *plain form*.)

Subject	S or P	Rule

1. Those worms (builds, build) tunnels in the ground.
2. They (is, are) fishing near the dam.
3. The doorbell (startles, startle) the baby.
4. The elephant herd (make, makes) its way through the jungle.
5. You (plays, play) the drums in our band.
6. The pictures (falls, fall) out of the album.
7. The astronomer (looks, look) through his telescope.

Exercise 6: In your journal, write a paragraph summarizing what you have learned this week.

Chapter 7 Test

Exercise 1: Classify each sentence.

1. _____ They cried at the end of the movie.

2. _____ Sit with them at the round table in the corner of the restaurant for excellent service.

3. _____ Jenny talked on her phone for a long time.

Exercise 2: Use Sentence 1 to underline the complete subject once and the complete predicate twice and to complete the table below.

List the Noun Used	List the Noun Job	Singular or Plural	Common or Proper	Simple Subject	Simple Predicate
1.	2.	3.	4.	5.	6.
7.	8.	9.	10.		

Exercise 3: Name the six parts of speech that you have studied. (*You may use abbreviations.*)

1. _____   2. _____   3. _____   4. _____   5. _____   6. _____

Exercise 4: Identify each pair of words as synonyms or antonyms by putting parentheses ( ) around **syn** or **ant**.

1. melt, congeal	syn ant	4. honest, truthful	syn ant	7. pain, discomfort	syn ant
2. present, absent	syn ant	5. burst, explode	syn ant	8. eager, indifferent	syn ant
3. try, attempt	syn ant	6. friend, foe	syn ant	9. kind, irreverent	syn ant

Exercise 5: For each sentence, write the subject, then write **S** if the subject is singular or **P** if the subject is plural, write the rule number, and underline the correct verb in the sentence.

Rule 1: A singular subject must use a singular verb form that ends in **s**: *is, was, has, does, or verbs ending with* **s** *or* **es**.
Rule 2: A plural subject, a compound subject, or the subject **YOU** must use a plural verb form that has **no s** ending: *are, were, do, have, or verbs without* **s** *or* **es** *endings.* (A plural verb form is also called the *plain form*.)

Subject	S or P	Rule

1. The water (rushes, rush) quickly down the brook.
2. Thomas and Angie (is, are) leaving for vacation.
3. My brothers (rides, ride) motorcycles.
4. That sculpture (are, is) new to the museum.
5. The dolphins (glides, glide) through the ocean water.
6. The hoses (was, were) tangled in a knot.
7. The new highway (curve, curves) through the hills.
8. (Do, Does) you know where Tammy lives?
9. The waitress (ask, asks) for our order.

Exercise 6: On notebook paper, write as many prepositions as you can.

Exercise 7: On notebook paper, write seven subject pronouns, seven possessive pronouns, and seven object pronouns.

Exercise 8: In your journal, write a paragraph summarizing what you have learned this week.

Chapter 8 Test

Exercise 1: Classify each sentence.

1. _____ The man's car broke down on the freeway yesterday.

2. _____ Our church's softball team played exceptionally well during the tournament.

3. _____ Think very carefully about the questions on the test.

Exercise 2: Use Sentence 1 to underline the complete subject once and the complete predicate twice and to complete the table below.

List the Noun Used	List the Noun Job	Singular or Plural	Common or Proper	Simple Subject	Simple Predicate
1.	2.	3.	4.	5.	6.
7.	8.	9.	10.		

Exercise 3: Name the six parts of speech that you have studied. (*You may use abbreviations.*)

1. _____   2. _____   3. _____   4. _____   5. _____   6. _____

Exercise 4: Identify each pair of words as synonyms or antonyms by putting parentheses ( ) around *syn* or *ant*.

1. fowl, chicken	syn ant	4. tame, savage	syn ant	7. accord, unity	syn ant
2. receive, send	syn ant	5. bland, tasty	syn ant	8. endangered, safe	syn ant
3. tempt, lure	syn ant	6. honest, truthful	syn ant	9. watch, vigil	syn ant

Exercise 5: Part A: Underline each noun to be made possessive and write singular or plural (**S-P**), the rule number, and the possessive form. Part B: Write each noun as singular possessive and then as plural possessive.

1. For a singular noun - add (**'s**)			2. For a plural noun that ends in *s* - add (**'**)		3. For a plural noun that does not end in *s* - add (**'s**)	
Rule 1: girl's			**Rule 2: girls'**		**Rule 3: women's**	

Part A	S-P	Rule	Possessive Form	Part B	Singular Poss	Plural Poss
1. pot handle				10. leaf		
2. authors ideas				11. bucket		
3. cows tails				12. pony		
4. orange peel				13. snake		
5. women slacks				14. yard		
6. Jason camera				15. driver		
7. flowers petals				16. child		
8. men suits				17. mouse		
9. children toys				18. video		

Exercise 6: On notebook paper, write seven subject pronouns, seven possessive pronouns, and seven object pronouns.

Exercise 7: In your journal, write a paragraph summarizing what you have learned this week.

Chapter 9 Test

Exercise 1: Classify each sentence.

1. _____ My family did not go on vacation during the summer.

2. _____ Did the pond freeze during the cold winter storm?

3. _____ We are riding on a bus to the party.

Exercise 2: Use Sentence 3 to underline the complete subject once and the complete predicate twice and to complete the table below.

List the Noun Used	List the Noun Job	Singular or Plural	Common or Proper	Simple Subject	Simple Predicate
1.	2.	3.	4.	5.	6.
7.	8.	9.	10.		

Exercise 3: Name the six parts of speech that you have studied. (*You may use abbreviations.*)

1. _____ 2. _____ 3. _____ 4. _____ 5. _____ 6. _____

Exercise 4: Identify each pair of words as synonyms or antonyms by putting parentheses ( ) around **syn** or **ant**.

1. accord, unity	syn ant	5. explode, burst	syn ant	9. fragrance, aroma	syn ant
2. rush, hurry	syn ant	6. timid, bold	syn ant	10. pain, discomfort	syn ant
3. cheap, costly	syn ant	7. tempt, lure	syn ant	11. endangered, safe	syn ant
4. friend, foe	syn ant	8. congeal, melt	syn ant	12. withdraw, join	syn ant

Exercise 5: For each sentence, write the subject, then write **S** if the subject is singular or **P** if the subject is plural, write the rule number (Rule 1 for singular and Rule 2 for plural), and underline the correct verb in the sentence.

Subject	S or P	Rule

1. The game (is, are) played on the grass.
2. Our windows (was, were) left open last night.
3. Angela and Joseph (writes, write) silly stories together.
4. The audience (claps, clap) at the marvelous act.
5. My chips (is, are) stale.
6. The flowers (was, were) sent in a vase.

Exercise 6: Part A: Underline each noun to be made possessive and write singular or plural (**S-P**), the rule number, and the possessive form. Part B: Write each noun as singular possessive and then as plural possessive.

1. For a singular noun - add (**'s**)			2. For a plural noun that ends in **s** - add (**'**)		3. For a plural noun that does not end in **s** - add (**'s**)	
Rule 1: girl's			Rule 2: girls'		Rule 3: women's	
Part A	**S-P**	**Rule**	**Possessive Form**	**Part B**	**Singular Poss**	**Plural Poss**
1. teacher desk				4. wife		
2. vine branch				5. cake		
3. men jobs				6. puppy		

Exercise 7: In your journal, write a paragraph summarizing what you have learned this week.

Chapter 10 Test

Exercise 1: Classify each sentence.

1. _____ Thomas and Andrew sang and danced at the talent show.

2. _____ Look at the colorful plants and fish in the large aquarium.

3. _____ Oops! The red juice spilled on the boy's white shirt.

Exercise 2: Use Sentence 2 to underline the complete subject once and the complete predicate twice and to complete the table below.

List the Noun Used	List the Noun Job	Singular or Plural	Common or Proper	Simple Subject	Simple Predicate
1.	2.	3.	4.	5.	6.
7.	8.	9.	10.		
11.	12.	13.	14.		

Exercise 3: Name the eight parts of speech that you have studied. (*You may use abbreviations.*)

1. _____ 2. _____ 3. _____ 4. _____ 5. _____ 6. _____ 7. _____ 8. _____

Exercise 4: Answer each question below.

1. List the 8 **be** verbs. _____
2. What are the parts of a verb phrase? _____
3. Name the seven subject pronouns. _____
4. Name the seven possessive pronouns. _____
5. Name the seven object pronouns. _____
6. What part of speech is the word NOT? _____

Exercise 5: Identify each pair of words as synonyms or antonyms by putting parentheses ( ) around **syn** or **ant**.

1. tepid, warm	syn ant	4. honest, truthful	syn ant	7. fragrance, aroma	syn ant
2. savage, tame	syn ant	5. serious, frivolous	syn ant	8. flabby, firm	syn ant
3. deadly, lethal	syn ant	6. wilt, droop	syn ant	9. scarce, abundant	syn ant

Exercise 6: Underline the correct homonym in each sentence.

1. He wants to (buy, by) my stamp collection.
2. I can't (weight, wait) for our summer break.
3. My sister ran (through, threw) the sprinkler.
4. My brothers (know, no) the owner of the restaurant.
5. My family left for a (weak, week) of vacation.
6. James gave money (to, too, two) the church.
7. She finally (one, won) the radio contest.
8. The university offered a summer (course, coarse).

Exercise 7: In your journal, write a paragraph summarizing what you have learned this week.

Chapter 11 Test

Exercise 1: Classify each sentence.

1. _____ Yea! The present from my grandparents arrived in the mail today!

2. _____ My brother fell down the steep stairs to the basement!

3. _____ Helen and her sister waited in the car in front of the store.

Exercise 2: Use Sentence 2 to underline the complete subject once and the complete predicate twice and to complete the table below.

List the Noun Used	List the Noun Job	Singular or Plural	Common or Proper	Simple Subject	Simple Predicate
1.	2.	3.	4.	5.	6.
7.	8.	9.	10.		
11.	12.	13.	14.		

Exercise 3: Name the eight parts of speech that you have studied. (*You may use abbreviations.*)

1. _____   2. _____   3. _____   4. _____   5. _____   6. _____   7. _____   8. _____

Exercise 4: Identify each pair of words as synonyms or antonyms by putting parentheses ( ) around **syn** or **ant**.

1. rush, hurry	syn ant	4. evade, avoid	syn ant	7. annoy, aggravate	syn ant
2. support, oppose	syn ant	5. bold, timid	syn ant	8. abundant, scarce	syn ant
3. droop, wilt	syn ant	6. tepid, warm	syn ant	9. intentional, unintended	syn ant

Exercise 5: Underline the correct homonym in each sentence.

1. Her made-up story was one big (tail, tale).
2. I drove her (knew, new) car today.
3. Those (too, two, to) girls stayed in the car.
4. We knew he was (to, too, two) friendly.
5. The dog yelped when I stepped on his (tail, tale).
6. We did not (here, hear) our mother's warning.
7. The boys found the arrowhead (here, hear).
8. The road that leads (to, two, too) town is steep.

Exercise 6: Use the Editing Guide below each sentence to know how many capitalization and punctuation errors to correct. For Sentence 1, write the capitalization and punctuation rule numbers for each correction in bold. For Sentence 2, make the capitalization and punctuation corrections. Use the capitalization and punctuation rule pages to help you.

> 1. **B**ro. **S**mith, **S**arah, and **S**imon were in charge of the **A**ugust report of the **N**ational **C**ouncil of **C**hurches.
>
>   **Editing Guide: Capitals: 8   Commas: 2   Periods: 1   End Marks: 1**
>
> 2. julies brother stephen won first place at the science fair in san francisco
>
>   **Editing Guide: Capitals: 4   Commas: 2   Apostrophes: 1   End Marks: 1**

Exercise 7: In your journal, write a paragraph summarizing what you have learned this week.

Chapter 12 Test A

Exercise 1: <u>Sentence</u>: Write the capitalization and punctuation rule numbers for each correction in bold.

1. **O**ur neighbor, **Mr. L. D. C**offee, was born across the **A**tlantic **O**cean in **P**aris, **F**rance.

Editing Guide: Capitals: 9	Commas: 3	Periods: 3	End Marks: 1

Exercise 2: <u>Friendly Letter</u>: Write the capitalization and punctuation corrections only.

113 calico drive

chateau tennessee 22006

june 6 20—

dear jonathan

    i heard that your science class was researching different kinds of animals i am able to obtain many helpful resources because i work with the tennessee game and fish commission i would be more than happy to send some of our booklets if you think they would be helpful in your research

affectionately yours

uncle james

Editing Guide: Capitals: 18	Commas: 4	End Marks: 3

Exercise 3: Name the eight parts of speech that you have studied. (*You may use abbreviations.*)

1. _____   2. _____   3. _____   4. _____   5. _____   6. _____   7. _____   8. _____

Exercise 4: Identify each pair of words as synonyms or antonyms by putting parentheses ( ) around *syn* or *ant*.

1. winner, victor	syn ant	4. tempt, lure	syn ant	7. annoy, aggravate	syn ant
2. depart, stay	syn ant	5. fragrance, aroma	syn ant	8. withdraw, join	syn ant
3. repaired, fixed	syn ant	6. evade, avoid	syn ant	9. unsightly, gorgeous	syn ant

Exercise 5: Underline the correct homonym in each sentence.

1. He prints with his (write, right) hand.
2. He (knew, new) this phone number.
3. The student (council, counsel) meets on Monday.
4. The skunk has a bad (scent, cent).
5. The quarterback (through, threw) a pass.
6. There are seven (daze, days) in a week.
7. Austin is the (capitol, capital) of Texas.
8. I think you (no, know) the correct answer.

Chapter 12 Test B

Exercise 1: Classify each sentence.

1. _____ Tina and Eric sat on the blanket in front of the television set.

2. _____ The sweet maple syrup dripped slowly down the side of the bottle.

3. _____ My youngest brother visited with the manager of the store.

Exercise 2: Sentence: Write the capitalization and punctuation corrections only.

1. thomas jenny and calvin visited the museum of natural science and history in tucson arizona

Editing Guide: Capitals: 9 Commas: 3 End Marks: 1

Exercise 3: Friendly Letter: Write the capitalization and punctuation rule numbers for each correction in bold.

233 **E**ast **S**alem **A**ve.

Mulvert **P**ass, **M**innesota 77009

January 10, 20—

Dear **M**ichelle,

We woke up to the most beautiful winter wonderland this morning. **T**he snow that covered the ground was at least three feet deep. **A**ll classes were cancelled. **J**ennifer and **I** played out in the snow all morning. **W**e spent the afternoon sipping hot cocoa and watching our favorite cartoons.

It really was a wonderful day!

Your cousin,

Julia

Editing Guide: Capitals: 18 Commas: 4 Periods: 1 End Marks: 6

Exercise 4: In your journal, write a paragraph summarizing what you have learned this week.

Chapter 13 Test

Exercise 1: Classify each sentence.

1. _____ The farmer feeds hay to his cows during the winter.

2. _____ Did the terrible windstorm damage tree branches and telephone lines?

3. _____ Does your family eat turkey and dressing during Thanksgiving?

Exercise 2: Use Sentence 1 to underline the complete subject once and the complete predicate twice and to complete the table below.

List the Noun Used	List the Noun Job	Singular or Plural	Common or Proper	Simple Subject	Simple Predicate
1.	2.	3.	4.	5.	6.
7.	8.	9.	10.		
11.	12.	13.	14.		
15.	16.	17.	18.		

Exercise 3: Identify each pair of words as synonyms or antonyms by putting parentheses ( ) around *syn* or *ant*.

1. tepid, warm	syn ant	4. support, oppose	syn ant	7. winner, victor	syn ant
2. repaired, fixed	syn ant	5. courage, fear	syn ant	8. pleasure, joy	syn ant
3. famous, obscure	syn ant	6. cover, wrap	syn ant	9. serious, frivolous	syn ant

Exercise 4: Underline the correct homonym in each sentence.
1. Can you (hear, here) the music on the radio?
2. We (lead, led) the music during service yesterday.
3. My arms felt (weak, week) from exhaustion.
4. The (lead, led) pipes made the drinking water unsafe.
5. Judy will be gone for a (weak, week).
6. They said (your, you're) from Ohio.
7. I really like (your, you're) new shoes.
8. Put your books over (hear, here).

Exercise 5: <u>For Sentences 1 and 2</u>: Write the capitalization and punctuation corrections only.
<u>For Sentence 3</u>: Write the capitalization and punctuation rule numbers for each correction in bold.

1. nancy is your recipe for c j s famous italian herb chicken an original from milan

> Editing Guide: Capitals: 5   Commas: 1   Apostrophes: 1   Periods: 2   End Marks: 1

2. today mrs rhines and i visited a famous indian reservation near cheyenne wyoming

> Editing Guide: Capitals: 7   Commas: 2   Periods: 1   End Marks: 1

3. **O**ur class president, **J. C. P**etty, announced this year's choir tour to **B**akersfield, **C**alifornia.

> Editing Guide: Capitals: 6   Commas: 3   Periods: 2   Apostrophes: 1   End Marks: 1

Exercise 6: In your journal, write a paragraph summarizing what you have learned this week.

Chapter 14 Test

Exercise 1: Classify each sentence.

1. _____ The campers built a cooking fire in the middle of their camp.

2. _____ Mark found some great bargains during the store's blowout sale.

Exercise 2: Use Sentence 2 to underline the complete subject once and the complete predicate twice and to complete the table below.

List the Noun Used	List the Noun Job	Singular or Plural	Common or Proper	Simple Subject	Simple Predicate
1.	2.	3.	4.	5.	6.
7.	8.	9.	10.		
11.	12.	13.	14.		

Exercise 3: Identify each pair of words as synonyms or antonyms by putting parentheses ( ) around **syn** or **ant**.

1. droop, wilt	syn ant	4. depart, stay	syn ant	7. consistent, irregular	syn ant
2. puny, robust	syn ant	5. evade, avoid	syn ant	8. smart, intelligent	syn ant
3. disease, illness	syn ant	6. pleasure, joy	syn ant	9. intentional, unintended	syn ant

Exercise 4: Put a slash to separate each run-on sentence below. Then, correct the run-on sentences by rewriting them on notebook paper as indicated by the labels in parentheses at the end of each sentence.

1. Daisies are blooming they cover the fields. (**CD**, and)
2. Johnny painted a picture Debbie painted a picture. (**SCS**)
3. The boys hung up a hammock they slept outside. (**SCV**)
4. My brother washed the dog he did not clean up the bathroom. (**CD**, but)
5. Timothy painted the fence Justin helped him. (**SCS**)
6. She laughed loudly she giggled loudly. (**SCV**)

Exercise 5: Identify each kind of sentence by writing the abbreviation in the blank. (**S, F, SCS, SCV, CD**).

_____ 1. Apples and pears are my favorite fruits.

_____ 2. The engine sputtered, and the lawnmower ran out of gas.

_____ 3. Walking through the city on a frigid winter morning.

_____ 4. The electrician switched off the breaker and repaired the broken wires.

_____ 5. The tiny baby tried to walk, but he toppled to the ground.

_____ 6. The detour around the construction site was very long.

_____ 7. I know her sister, but I can't remember her name.

Exercise 6: On notebook paper, write two sentences, using these labels to guide you: (**SCV**) (**CD**, and).

Exercise 7: In your journal, write a paragraph summarizing what you have learned this week.

Chapter 15 Test

Exercise 1: Classify each sentence.

1. _____ Tommy and Daniel have landed the plane safely on the runway at the airport.

2. _____ Pass the peanuts and popcorn to me.

Exercise 2: Use Sentence 2 to underline the complete subject once and the complete predicate twice and to complete the table below.

List the Noun Used	List the Noun Job	Singular or Plural	Common or Proper	Simple Subject	Simple Predicate
1.	2.	3.	4.	5.	6.
7.	8.	9.	10.		

Exercise 3: Identify each pair of words as synonyms or antonyms by putting parentheses ( ) around **syn** or **ant**.

1. disease, illness	syn ant	4. cover, wrap	syn ant	7. smart, intelligent	syn ant
2. censor, permit	syn ant	5. distant, remote	syn ant	8. hidden, concealed	syn ant
3. famous, obscure	syn ant	6. occupied, vacant	syn ant	9. gorgeous, unsightly	syn ant

Exercise 4: Put a slash to separate each run-on sentence below. Then, correct the run-on sentences by rewriting them on notebook paper as indicated by the labels in parentheses at the end of each sentence.

1. The birds are flying south they cover the sky. **(CD, and)**
2. Erin studied for the exam Jack studied for the exam. **(SCS)**
3. The girls sat at the kitchen table they ate banana splits. **(SCV)**
4. The artist made many sculptures he did not sell them at the market. **(CD, but)**

Exercise 5: Identify each kind of sentence by writing the abbreviation in the blank. (**S, F, SCS, SCV, CD**).

_____ 1. Tina and Jerry ran to catch the bus.

_____ 2. The car put on its blinker and turned off the highway.

_____ 3. Wading in the creek behind my grandmother's house.

_____ 4. The customers waited in line and paid their bills.

_____ 5. The young lady carried her briefcase, but she forgot her keys.

_____ 6. The frog jumped onto the lily pad.

_____ 7. Joe quickly went to the bank, and he made a large deposit for his company.

Exercise 6: Copy the following words on notebook paper. Write the correct contraction beside each word. **Words:** cannot, let us, do not, was not, they are, are not, had not, is not, she is, who is, you are, did not, it is, we are, were not, does not, has not, I am, I have, I had, will not, I will, would not, I would, should not, could not, they would.

Exercise 7: In your journal, write a paragraph summarizing what you have learned this week.

Chapter 16 Test

Exercise 1: Classify each sentence.

1. _____ Yikes! The three ferocious beasts showed their sharp fangs to the dangerous cougar!

2. _____ We are taking ham and cheese sandwiches on the picnic.

Exercise 2: Use Sentence 1 to underline the complete subject once and the complete predicate twice and to complete the table below.

List the Noun Used	List the Noun Job	Singular or Plural	Common or Proper	Simple Subject	Simple Predicate
1.	2.	3.	4.	5.	6.
7.	8.	9.	10.		
11.	12.	13.	14.		

Exercise 3: Identify each pair of words as synonyms or antonyms by putting parentheses ( ) around *syn* or *ant*.

1. offer, volunteer	syn ant	4. pretend, imagine	syn ant	7. sparse, plentiful	syn ant
2. distant, remote	syn ant	5. fear, courage	syn ant	8. consistent, irregular	syn ant
3. sorrow, bliss	syn ant	6. hidden, concealed	syn ant	9. occupied, vacant	syn ant

Exercise 4: Tell whether each sentence contains a simile or a metaphor by writing *like* or *as* in the Simile column or by writing the noun in the predicate that renames the subject in the Metaphor column.

	Simile	Metaphor
1. My uncle is as unpredictable as the weather.		
2. My cousin is a walking encyclopedia.		
3. My father is a bear before his morning coffee.		
4. Shelly looked like an angel in the morning light.		
5. My brother stood as still as a statue.		

Exercise 5: Underline each subject and fill in each column according to the title.

	List each Verb	Write PrN, PA, or None	Write L or A
1. Bats are mammals.			
2. Sirens screamed across town.			
3. Our daughter is the class treasurer.			
4. His new shirt is torn.			
5. The mailman was friendly yesterday.			
6. Her hair is too curly.			

Exercise 6: On notebook paper, write one sentence for each of these labels: **(SCS)**, **(SCV)**, **(CD)**.

Exercise 7: In your journal, write a paragraph summarizing what you have learned this week.

Level 3—Shurley English—Homeschool Edition

Chapter 17 Test

Exercise 1: Classify each sentence.

1. _____ Cindy's baby boy had a red rash on his skin.

2. _____ The young seal splashed into the cold ocean water.

Exercise 2: Use Sentence 2 to underline the complete subject once and the complete predicate twice and to complete the table below.

List the Noun Used	List the Noun Job	Singular or Plural	Common or Proper	Simple Subject	Simple Predicate
1.	2.	3.	4.	5.	6.
7.	8.	9.	10.		

Exercise 3: Identify each pair of words as synonyms or antonyms by putting parentheses ( ) around *syn* or *ant*.

1. alike, identical	syn ant	4. slope, incline	syn ant	7. offer, volunteer	syn ant
2. tidy, cluttered	syn ant	5. puny, robust	syn ant	8. guarded, unprotected	syn ant
3. censor, permit	syn ant	6. pretend, imagine	syn ant	9. plentiful, sparse	syn ant

Exercise 4: Use the Quotation Rules to help punctuate the quotations below. Underline the explanatory words.

1. where did you find those earrings i asked beth

2. beth answered mrs matthews got these for me at ralphs gift store on prince street

3. they are absolutely gorgeous i exclaimed

4. beth smiled and said ill be sure to tell mrs matthews that you like them

Exercise 5: Copy the following contractions on notebook paper. Write the correct word beside each contraction.
Contractions: can't, let's, don't, wasn't, they're, aren't, hadn't, isn't, she's, who's, you're, didn't, it's, we're.

Exercise 6: On notebook paper, write one sentence for each of these labels: **(SCS) (SCV) (CD, and)**.

Exercise 7: On notebook paper, write a sentence demonstrating a beginning quote and a sentence demonstrating an end quote.

Exercise 8: In your journal, write a paragraph summarizing what you have learned this week.

Level 3 Homeschool Student Book

Test Section - Page 113

© SHURLEY INSTRUCTIONAL MATERIALS, INC.

Chapter 18 Test A

Exercise 1: Classify each sentence.

1. _____ Does the liquid in a thermometer go up or down during cold weather?

2. _____ Oh no! My brother found his birthday present in the hall closet!

Exercise 2: Use Sentence 2 to underline the complete subject once and the complete predicate twice and to complete the table below.

List the Noun Used	List the Noun Job	Singular or Plural	Common or Proper	Simple Subject	Simple Predicate
1.	2.	3.	4.	5.	6.
7.	8.	9.	10.		
11.	12.	13.	14.		

Exercise 3: Identify each pair of words as synonyms or antonyms by putting parentheses ( ) around **syn** or **ant**.

1. strange, unusual	syn ant	4. crack, crevice	syn ant	7. identical, alike	syn ant
2. sorrow, bliss	syn ant	5. defeat, victory	syn ant	8. guarded, unprotected	syn ant
3. allow, thwart	syn ant	6. censor, permit	syn ant	9. concealed, hidden	syn ant

Exercise 4: Underline each verb or verb phrase. Identify the verb tense by writing a number **1** for present tense, a number **2** for past tense, or a number **3** for future tense. Write the past tense form and **R** or **I** for Regular or Irregular.

Verb Tense		Main Verb Past Tense Form	R or I
	1. He is traveling to Europe.		
	2. The students will make our lunch.		
	3. Was she searching for the recipe?		
	4. The ducks are flying south for the winter.		
	5. The principal had called his mother.		
	6. Debby will slice the apples.		
	7. Cody talked to the counselor.		
	8. We have sold all the tickets.		
	9. Jacob is swimming in our pool.		
	10. Katy was throwing the baseball.		

Exercise 5: Identify each kind of sentence by writing the abbreviation in the blank. (**S, F, SCS, SCV, CD**).

_____ 1. She picked the apples, and her mother baked them.

_____ 2. We mowed the lawn and watered the flowers.

_____ 3. Fruits and vegetables should be eaten everyday.

_____ 4. During the contest.

_____ 5. He called his grandmother, and they talked for hours.

Chapter 18 Test B

Exercise 6: Change the underlined present tense verbs in Paragraph 1 to past tense verbs in Paragraph 2.

Paragraph 1: Present Tense

    Mr. Chang **performs** many jobs at his restaurant. First, he **buys** fresh meats and vegetables. He **selects** only the finest ingredients to be prepared. Later, he **helps** out in the kitchen. Mr. Chang **dices** vegetables into small pieces for the cooks. He also **greets** his customers with a smile. He always **checks** for customer satisfaction. Mr. Chang **wears** many hats at his restaurant.

Paragraph 2: Past Tense

    Mr. Chang _____ many jobs at his restaurant. First, he _____ fresh meats and vegetables. He _____ only the finest ingredients to be prepared. Later, he _____ out in the kitchen. Mr. Chang _____ vegetables into small pieces for the cooks. He also _____ his customers with a smile. He always _____ for customer satisfaction. Mr. Chang _____ many hats at his restaurant.

Exercise 7: Change the underlined mixed tense verbs in Paragraph 1 to present tense verbs in Paragraph 2.

Paragraph 1: Mixed Tense

    My sister and I **went** to the park every weekend. We **laugh** and **played** for hours on the swings. She **pushes** me high into the sky, and I **screamed** loudly! Sometimes, I **push** her on the merry-go-round. She always **begged** me to slow down. My sister and I **run** and **played** happily at the park every weekend.

Paragraph 2: Present Tense

    My sister and I _____ to the park every weekend. We _____ and _____ for hours on the swings. She _____ me high into the sky, and I _____ loudly! Sometimes, I _____ her on the merry-go-round. She always _____ me to slow down. My sister and I _____ and _____ happily at the park every weekend.

Exercise 8: On notebook paper, write the seven present tense helping verbs, the five past tense helping verbs, and the two future tense helping verbs.

Exercise 9: In your journal, write a paragraph summarizing what you have learned this week.

Chapter 19 Test

Exercise 1: Classify each sentence.

1. _____ Wow! Bill's brother has been running in the marathon for two hours!

2. _____ Did you spill the cereal on the kitchen floor?

3. _____ Henry sorted the dirty clothes in the laundry basket.

Exercise 2: Identify each pair of words as synonyms or antonyms by putting parentheses **( )** around *syn* or *ant*.

1. incline, slope	syn ant	4. perceptive, insightful	syn ant	7. thwart, allow	syn ant
2. public, private	syn ant	5. construct, destroy	syn ant	8. cluttered, tidy	syn ant
3. crack, crevice	syn ant	6. rejoice, celebrate	syn ant	9. victory, defeat	syn ant

Exercise 3: Change the underlined mixed tense verbs in Paragraph 1 to past tense verbs in Paragraph 2.

Paragraph 1: Mixed Tenses

Yesterday, Jerry and I **went** to the zoo. Jerry **loves** the monkey cages, so we **walked** to them first. He **imitated** the monkeys' calls, and we both **laugh**. When the day **was** almost over, we **walk** back to the car and **left**.

Paragraph 2: Past Tense

Yesterday, Jerry and I _____ to the zoo. Jerry _____

the monkey cages, so we _____ to them first. He _____ the monkeys' calls, and we both

_____. When the day _____

almost over, we _____ back to the car and _____.

Exercise 4: Underline the negative words in each sentence. Rewrite each sentence on notebook paper and correct the double negative mistake as indicated by the rule number in parentheses at the end of the sentence.

Rule 1	Rule 2	Rule 3
Change the second negative to a positive.	Take out the negative part of a contraction.	Remove the first negative word (verb change).

1. Barry doesn't have no razors. (Rule 1)   3. My dad doesn't have no neckties. (Rule 3)

2. I can't never find any toothbrush. (Rule 2)   4. He isn't never home. (Rule 2)

Exercise 5: Copy the following words on notebook paper. Write the correct contraction beside each word.
Words: you have, there is, is not, they will, will not, it is, he will, let us, we would, I will.

Exercise 6: Copy the following contractions on notebook paper. Write the correct word beside each contraction.
Contractions: they're, he's, you're, hasn't, you'd, we've, doesn't, hadn't, can't, I'd, don't.

Exercise 7: In your journal, write a paragraph summarizing what you have learned this week.

Chapter 20 Test

Exercise 1: Classify each sentence.

1. _____ We built a large snowman in our neighbor's yard.

2. _____ The guests sneaked into Eve's house for a surprise party!

Exercise 2: Identify each pair of words as synonyms or antonyms by putting parentheses ( ) around **syn** or **ant**.

1. sorrow, bliss	syn ant	4. unusual, strange	syn ant	7. construct, destroy	syn ant
2. excuse, alibi	syn ant	5. delete, insert	syn ant	8. insightful, perceptive	syn ant
3. public, private	syn ant	6. hesitate, pause	syn ant	9. effortless, laborious	syn ant

Exercise 3: Write the rule number from Reference 60 and the correct plural form of the nouns below.

	Rule	Plural Form			Rule	Plural Form
1. key				6. brush		
2. pansy				7. child		
3. mouse				8. moose		
4. cameo				9. wolf		
5. knife				10. whiff		

Exercise 4: Underline the negative words in each sentence. Rewrite each sentence on notebook paper and correct the double negative mistake as indicated by the rule number in parentheses at the end of the sentence.

Rule 1	Rule 2	Rule 3
Change the second negative to a positive.	Take out the negative part of a contraction.	Remove the first negative word (verb change).

1. The car doesn't have no gas. (Rule 3)

2. She wouldn't eat no cereal. (Rule 2)

3. Sandra shouldn't eat no dessert. (Rule 1)

4. The teacher didn't never give the test. (Rule 3)

5. That guide didn't bring no water. (Rule 1)

6. Scott hasn't never stayed out late. (Rule 2)

Exercise 5: On notebook paper, write the seven present tense helping verbs, the five past tense helping verbs, and the two future tense helping verbs.

Exercise 6: Copy the following words on notebook paper. Write the correct contraction beside each word. **Words:** cannot, let us, do not, was not, they are, are not, had not, is not, she is, who is, you are, did not, it is.

Exercise 7: In your journal, write a paragraph summarizing what you have learned this week.

Chapter 21 Test

Exercise 1: Classify each sentence.

1. _____ Ride your bicycle on the sidewalk in front of the house.

2. _____ Oh, no! Her new red ball rolled in front of the fast cars on the highway!

Exercise 2: Identify each pair of words as synonyms or antonyms by putting parentheses ( ) around **syn** or **ant**.

1. torrid, frigid	syn ant	4. allow, thwart	syn ant	7. hesitate, pause	syn ant
2. insert, delete	syn ant	5. most, maximum	syn ant	8. sudden, abrupt	syn ant
3. excuse, alibi	syn ant	6. link, disconnect	syn ant	9. laborious, effortless	syn ant

Exercise 3: Underline the negative words in each sentence. Rewrite each sentence on notebook paper and correct the double negative mistake as indicated by the rule number in parentheses at the end of the sentence.

Rule 1	Rule 2	Rule 3
Change the second negative to a positive.	Take out the negative part of a contraction.	Remove the first negative word (verb change).

1. Our cattle won't eat no hay. (Rule 1)   4. She doesn't do nothing after school. (Rule 3)

2. The waitress didn't want no tip. (Rule 1)   5. He wouldn't never be late for work. (Rule 2)

3. My uncle didn't never visit us. (Rule 3)   6. You shouldn't never borrow money. (Rule 2)

Exercise 4: Write the rule number from Reference 60 and the correct plural form of the nouns below.

	Rule	Plural Form			Rule	Plural Form
1. convoy			6. tax			
2. berry			7. louse			
3. postman			8. sheep			
4. rodeo			9. calf			
5. half			10. cliff			

Exercise 5: On notebook paper, write the seven present tense helping verbs, the five past tense helping verbs, and the two future tense helping verbs.

Exercise 6: Copy the following words on notebook paper. Write the correct contraction beside each word. **Words:** cannot, let us, do not, was not, they are, are not, had not, is not, she is, who is, you are, did not, it is, we are, were not, does not, has not, I am, I have, I would, will not, I will, would not, should not, could not, they would.

Exercise 7: In your journal, write a paragraph summarizing what you have learned this week.

Chapter 22 Test

Exercise 1: Classify each sentence.

1. _____ Do kindergarten children take a nap after lunch?

2. _____ Lillian and Bryan shoveled the snow off the driveway yesterday.

Exercise 2: Identify each pair of words as synonyms or antonyms by putting parentheses ( ) around *syn* or *ant*.					
1. fad, craze	syn ant	4. link, disconnect	syn ant	7. rejoice, celebrate	syn ant
2. torrid, frigid	syn ant	5. most, maximum	syn ant	8. abrupt, sudden	syn ant
3. evil, wicked	syn ant	6. offend, compliment	syn ant	9. educated, illiterate	syn ant

Exercise 3: Use the Quotation Rules to help punctuate the quotations below. Underline the explanatory words.

1. donna would you like to eat at morrisons cafeteria i asked

2. denise shouted loudly to adam and daniel look out for that car

3. i would like to visit mrs thompson today jessica said to her mother

4. the shy girl spoke softly i havent finished my book report mr jones

5. that alligator was ten feet long gasped patrick to his brother

Exercise 4: On notebook paper, tell what you have learned about the business letter and the business letter envelope

Exercise 5: On notebook paper, tell what you have learned about the friendly letter and the friendly letter envelope.

Exercise 6: In your journal, write a paragraph summarizing what you have learned this week.

Chapter 23 Test

Exercise 1: Classify each sentence.

1. _____ Ship the package to my home in Florida.

2. _____ Look! The policeman is firing a warning shot in the air!

Exercise 2: Match each part of a book listed below with the type of information it may give you. Write the appropriate letter in the blank. You may use each letter only once.

| A. Body | B. Preface | C. Bibliography | D. Index | E. Copyright page |
| F. Title Page | G. Appendix | | | |

1. _____ Exact page numbers for a particular topic and used to locate topics quickly

2. _____ Text of the book

3. _____ Reason the book was written

4. _____ Books listed for finding more information

5. _____ ISBN number

6. _____ Publisher's name and city where the book was published

7. _____ Extra maps in a book

Exercise 3: Underline the correct answers.

1. Nonfiction books contain information and stories that are (**true   not true**).
2. Fiction books contain information and stories that are (**true   not true**).
3. The main reference book that is primarily a book of maps is the
   (**encyclopedia   dictionary   atlas   almanac**).
4. The main reference book that gives the definition, spelling, and pronunciation of words
   is the (**encyclopedia   dictionary   atlas   almanac**).
5. The main reference book that is published once a year with a variety of up-to-date information
   is the (**encyclopedia   dictionary   atlas   almanac**).
6. What would you find by going to *The Readers' Guide to Periodical Literature*?
   (**newspaper articles   magazine articles   encyclopedia articles**)

Exercise 4: On notebook paper, write the five parts found at the front of a book.

Exercise 5: On notebook paper, write the four parts found at the back of a book.

Exercise 6: In your journal, write a paragraph summarizing what you have learned this week.

Chapter 24 Test

Exercise 1: Classify each sentence.

1. _____ Did   your   dad   build   those   shelves   in   the   den?

2. _____ Sue's   sister   drove   with   her   cousin   to   the   museum.

Exercise 2: Put each group of words in alphabetical order. Use numbers to show the order in each column.

Winter Words	Picnic Words	"D" Words	Kitchen Words	"G" Words
____ 1. ice	____ 5. food	____ 9. date	____ 13. sink	____ 17. gang
____ 2. cold	____ 6. blanket	____ 10. dull	____ 14. dishes	____ 18. ground
____ 3. snow	____ 7. ants	____ 11. deep	____ 15. table	____ 19. germ
____ 4. freeze	____ 8. summer	____ 12. defend	____ 16. oven	____ 20. gas

Exercise 3: Below are the tops of two dictionary pages. Write the page number on which each word listed would appear.

kingly (first word)	Page 398	**knew** (last word)		**knife** (first word)	Page 399	**knot** (last word)

Page	Page	Page	Page
____ 1. kiss	____ 3. knit	____ 5. knee	____ 7. knock
____ 2. knight	____ 4. kite	____ 6. kit	____ 8. kitten

Exercise 4: Match the definitions of the parts of a dictionary entry below. Write the correct letter of the word beside each definition.

_____ 1. gives correct spelling and divides the word into syllables.   A.   pronunciation

_____ 2. sentences using the entry word to illustrate a meaning   B.   meanings

_____ 3. numbered definitions listed according to the part of speech   C.   entry word

_____ 4. shows how to pronounce a word, usually put in parentheses   D.   synonyms

_____ 5. small *n.* for noun, small *v.* for verb, *adj.* for adjective, etc.   E.   parts of speech

_____ 6. words that have similar meanings to the entry word   F.   examples

Exercise 5: In your journal, write a paragraph summarizing what you have learned this week.